THE GREAT BOOK OF HAWAII

The Crazy History of Hawaii with Amazing Random Facts & Trivia

A Trivia Nerds Guide to the History of the United States Vol.7

BILL O'NEILL

ISBN: 978-1-64845-008-2

DON'T FORGET YOUR
FREE BOOKS

GET THEM FOR FREE ON
WWW.TRIVIABILL.COM

CONTENTS

CHAPTER TWO
HAWAII'S MAIN ISLANDS AND OTHER
FACTS ABOUT THE STATE 31

CHAPTER THREE
HAWAII'S POPCULTURE AND SPORTS...............58

CHAPTER FOUR
HAWAII'S INVENTIONS, IDEAS, AND MORE!...84

CHAPTER FIVE

HAWAII'S ATTRACTIONS...................................... 105

CHAPTER SIX
HAWAII'S UNSOLVED MYSTERIES, URBAN LEGENDS, AND OTHER WEIRD FACTS 130

INTRODUCTION

What do you know about the state of Hawaii?

Sure, you know it's paradise. You know it's a popular honeymoon destination and a popular bucket list item for many. But do you know which Hawaiian island is visited most frequently? Do you know how Hawaii got its name or why it's called the "Aloha State"?

You're probably familiar with the eight main islands, but do you know how many islands there are altogether? Did you know that each of the Hawaiian main islands has a nickname of its own?

Do you know about Hawaii's royal past or how it became the state we know it as today?

You probably already know Hawaii is home to volcanoes, but how much do you really know about them?

Do you know about Hawaii's many inventions, which range from a famous sport to a stringed instrument?

Do you know about some of the most interesting legends in the ancient Hawaiian culture? Have you heard of one of the most famous goddesses in Hawaiian mythology and some of the legends about her?

If you have ever wondered about the answers to these or other questions about Hawaii, then you've come to the right place. This isn't just any book about Hawaii. It's filled with interesting stories and facts about the Aloha State. Whether you're a lifelong resident of Hawaii or you've never set foot in the state, you're bound to learn something new. Once you've finished reading, you'll know so much about the Aloha State that you'll even impress your history teacher!

Hawaii is a state that's rich in both history and culture. We'll bounce around some as we take a closer look at some of the most interesting historical facts about the Aloha State. You'll learn more about the main islands, Hawaiian pop culture, sports, and so much more!

This book is broken up into easy to follow chapters that will help you learn more about the Aloha State. Then we'll find out how much attention you've been paying with trivia questions at the end of every chapter.

Some of the facts you'll read about are shocking. Some of them are weird and others are fun. But there's one thing all of these facts have in common: they're *all* interesting! Once you have finished this book, you're guaranteed to walk away with a wealth of knowledge about the Aloha State.

As an added bonus, you'll learn the meanings of several words from the Hawaiian language along the way!

This book will answer the following questions:

How did Hawaii get its name?

Why is it called the Aloha State?

Why was it once called "The Kingdom of Hawaii"?

What is each of the main islands nicknamed?

Which sport was invented in Hawaii?

Which movies have been filmed in the state?

Which famous actress got her start thanks to her role as an extra in a movie filmed in Hawaii?

What legends from the Hawaiian culture haunt the state?

What's Hawaii's most famous unsolved mystery?

And so much more!

CHAPTER ONE

HAWAII'S HISTORY AND RANDOM FACTS

In August of 1959, Hawaii became the 50th—and final—state to join the union. This happened when 93% of Americans voted in favor of a proposition that would admit the territory as a state. Hawaii's addition to the union happened the same year that Alaska became a state. How much do you know about the state's history? Do you know what makes it unique and different from the rest of the United States? Do you know how the state got its nickname? Do you know which former President of the United States was born in Hawaii? Read on to learn some of the most interesting facts about the history of the Aloha State!

How Hawaii Got Its Name

Have you ever wondered how the state came to be known as "Hawaii"? While it's not entirely known how the state got its name, there are a few different theories. But first, let's start from the beginning— when Hawaii was named something else first!

The Hawaiian Islands were settled by Polynesians more than 1,000 years ago. It's been estimated that some of the first Polynesian settlements began sometime between the 10th and 13th century.

It wasn't until the 1700s that the islands were discovered by Europeans.

Back in 1778, Captain James Cook became the first European on record to discover the Hawaiian Islands. Cook named the islands the "Sandwich Islands." He chose this name in honor of the Earl of Sandwich. The name for the islands didn't last long, however, as the islands eventually became known as the Kingdom of Hawaii. But where exactly did Hawaii come from?

Well, that's where things aren't entirely clear. The state of Hawaii got its name from the island of Hawaii, which is one of the state's eight main islands. But no one knows for sure how the island of Hawaii got its name.

The most popular theory is based on an ancient Hawaiian legend, which says that the island was named after the first Polynesian explorer to settle on the island. This early settler was said to be a man by the name of Hawaii Loa (or Hawai'iloa). According to the legend, Hawaii Loa was a fisherman who stumbled on the island while he was out with a crew of his men. The island was allegedly named after him. Hawaii Loa is said to have left the island and later returned with his family.

Although many modern Hawaiians accept the story of Hawaii Loa as an accurate depiction of how the islands were settled, others question if it's nothing more than a myth. In some of the earliest ancient Hawaiian history books, there's no mention of Hawaii Loa. So, if this tale isn't true, then where did the island of Hawaii actually get its name?

Another theory is that the word came from the Polynesian words "Hawa" and "ii." Hawa means "traditional homeland" and ii means "small." Combined, these two words mean "small homeland."

It's also believed that the word may have originated from the Proto-Polynesian word Hawaiki, which means "place of the Gods" or "homeland."

Hawaii Was Once Known as "The Kingdom of Hawaii"

Did you know that Hawaii is the only U.S. state that was once an independent monarchy? In fact, it was actually known as "The Kingdom of Hawaii" at one point in time! It might be hard to imagine the state as we know it today as a kingdom in the past, but it was.

Three years after Captain James Cook was killed over a dispute over a longboat, Kīwalaʻō, became the King of the Island of Hawaii. Religious rule of the island was given to his nephew, Kamehameha. Chiefs supported Kamehameha, which led to a war to overthrow Kīwalaʻō. Kīwalaʻō was killed during a battle.

By 1795, Kamehameha I, who's also sometimes referred to as Kamehameha the Great, had formed the Kingdom of Hawaii. He had succeeded in winning Oahu and Maui in battles, but he lost the battle in Kauai. In 1810, however, the islands of Kauai and Niihau agreed to join the Kingdom of Hawaii instead of going to war. This led to the unification of the entire Hawaiian archipelago.

The Kamehameha Dynasty, otherwise known as the House of Kamehameha, was the longest family to reign in the monarchy. The family's dynasty continued until the deaths of Kamehameha V in 1872 and William Charles Lunalilo (the highest chief and first monarch to be elected into the Kingdom of Hawaii under the Kamehameha Dynasty) in 1874.

The Kalakaua Dynasty, or the House of Kalakaua, was the next to rule the Kingdom of Hawaii. King David Kalakaua was elected to the throne after the males of the Kamehameha Dynasty died out.

The Kalakaua Dynasty lasted until 1893 when Queen Liliuokalani was overthrown.

Bonus Fact: Today, you might see the word Ali'i a lot when it comes to the Kingdom of Hawaii's former rules. This is because *Ali'i* means "a hereditary line of rulers." Ali'i might be used when referring to a king, chief, queen or other noble.

The Hawaiian Monarchy Was Overthrown by the United States

When Liliuokalani became Queen of the Kingdom of Hawaii after her brother King Kalakaua's death, she proposed a new constitution. The constitution would give voting rights to Hawaii's natives, as well as restore powers of the monarchy.

Needless to say, many of the white businessmen residing in Hawaii were angered by the Queen's proposal. Thirteen of them formed the Committee of Public Safety. Their goal was to overthrow the Queen and seek annexation by the United States.

In January of 1893, the Committee of Public Safety gathered near the Iolani Palace where the Queen lived. John L. Stevens, who was the U.S. Minister of Hawaii, had ordered more than 160 U.S. Navy sailors and Marines to protect them.

In order to avoid violence, Queen Liliuokalani surrendered.

A provisional government was established by the Committee of Public Safety, but United States

President Grover Cleveland ordered that Queen Liliuokalani be restored to power. However, the Committee of Public Safety formed the Republic of Hawaii anyway, refusing to give up their power.

In 1895, a group of Hawaii's royals tried to form a coup against the Republic of Hawaii. They were unsuccessful, however. Queen Liliuokalani was a part of that movement. She was convicted of treason and sentenced to house arrest.

When Queen Liliuokalani was under house arrest, she agreed to formally abdicated and dissolve Hawaii's monarchy.

Hawaii was annexed by the United States in 1898. It was a U.S. territory until 1959 when it finally became a state.

Hawaii is the Only State with a Palace

Due to its history as the only state with an independent monarchy, it may come as no surprise for you to learn that Hawaii is also the only state with a palace. It also has not just one but *two* palaces!

Iolani Palace, which is located in Honolulu, plays a key role in Hawaii's history. The palace was home to several of the Kingdom of Hawaii's rulers. The first to live in the palace was King Kamehameha III under the Kamehameha Dynasty. The last ruler to live in Iolani Palace was Queen Liliuokalani under the Kalakaua Dynasty.

Today, Iolani Palace is a National Historic Landmark and museum that preserves the state's royal history. The palace has gone through a number of changes since it was home to the Royals. It was used as the capitol building up until 1969. During the late 1970s, the palace was restored to its original beauty.

The Hulihee Palace can also be found in Hawaii. Located in Kailua-Kona, Hawaii, the palace once served as a vacation home to the Royals. Today, it serves as a museum.

How Hawaii Came to be Known as the Aloha State

Hawaii is officially nicknamed the "Aloha State." The nickname was chosen because "Aloha" is one of the most common words that's spoken in the Hawaiian language. Aloha is used to say "hello," "welcome," "love," "best wishes," and "goodbye." Hawaiians are known to be very friendly and often use the word as a greeting for both friends and strangers.

In Hawaiian culture, it's thought that one should practice the "spirit of Aloha." This goes beyond just greetings. It's considered to be a way of life. The idea is that one should always practice kindness, compassion, harmony, and humility. It's about giving the shirt off your back to someone in need or holding the door for strangers. This is another one of the reasons why Hawaii was given its nickname.

Although Hawaii is officially nicknamed the Aloha State, there are a number of unofficial nicknames that are also used to describe the state. These include:

- The "Pineapple State" – This nickname is used because 1/3 of pineapples produced throughout the world come from Hawaii.
- The "Paradise of the Pacific" – The state's natural beauty and its location make this nickname a self-explanatory one.
- The "Youngest State" – It's sometimes called this since it's the last state to join the Union.

Hawaii is Made Up of More Than Eight Islands

Hawaii is well-known for its eight main islands. These islands, from largest to smallest, are:

1. Hawaii
2. Maui
3. Oahu
4. Kauai
5. Molokai
6. Lanai
7. Niihau
8. Kahoolawe

But did you know that there are actually more than just eight islands in the state of Hawaii? In fact, there are 132 islands that make up the state! The other 124 islands are islets, reefs, and shoals. None of these other islands have residents, however.

Fun fact: Hawaii is the only state in the U.S. that's compromised entirely of islands!

One Hawaiian Island Once Served as a Leper Colony

Hawaii's islands weren't always sunshine and rainbows. In fact, one of its islands has an incredibly tragic past.

Back in 1866, leprosy was spreading rapidly throughout Hawaii. The disease was first introduced to the islands by traders, sailors, workers, and other people from Eurasia, where the disease was common at the time. Sugar planters were worried about the toll leprosy would take on their workforce and pressured the Hawaiian government to do something to stop the disease from spreading.

With no cure in sight, more than 100 people were shipped to Kalawao, a leper colony that was established on the island of Molokai's Kalaupapa peninsula.

Kalawao was used as a leper colony from 1866 to 1969, beginning with the Kingdom of Hawaii until the region was a U.S. territory. During that time, more than 8,500 Hawaiian men, women, and children who were diagnosed with leprosy were taken to the colony to be quarantined and, ultimately, die. Upon arrival, they were all legally declared dead, though many lived in the settlement after their diagnosis. At one point, the settlement had around 1,100 members. Many people even chose to continue to live in the settlement even after medication became available to treat the disease.

As of 2015, there were still six patients who remained from the leprosy colony who lived on Molokai. There's no reason to believe that there's any risk of contracting the disease on the island, however.

Leis Have an Interesting History in Hawaii

When you visit any of the Hawaiian Islands today, you'll be given a lei—or a wreath of flowers—when you arrive on the island and when you leave the island. This is because leis have become a popular gesture of affection. The iconic lei plays a key role in Hawaii's tourism. But did you know that leis actually have historical significance in Hawaii as well?

In ancient times, the tradition of leis was brought to the region by the Polynesians. Native Hawaiians gave leis to their chiefs as a sign of affection. Chiefs also would make peace within another by weaving leis together.

Native Hawaiians also wore leis that represented their ranks within society. The Royals wore different lei colors than the commoners. It was possible to move up within the ranks and change lei colors based on class changes. This was a way for ancient Hawaiians to know who to show the most respect to. Chiefs, of course, were always most highly respected.

Historically, leis were also commonly worn by hula dancers.

So, where did the idea of giving leis to tourists come from? Rumor has it that a hula dancer once gave a lei to a U.S. soldier, along with a kiss, during World War II. This allegedly led to the idea of distributing leis to anyone who came to the island. Whether this story is true or not, it's important to remember that it's an honor to receive a lei. Leis are considered a significant part of native Hawaiian culture and should be treated with respect. There are a number of etiquette rules to keep in mind regarding leis. Here are some rules to keep in mind:

1. It's considered impolite to refuse a lei that's being given to you. If you have allergies, you should express this to the giver. You should also leave it at your seat or carry it with you, if possible.
2. It's thought to be rude to remove a lei in front of the person who gave it to you.
3. It's not acceptable to wear a lei that you plan to give to someone else.
4. You should never throw a lei away. It should be returned to the earth and, if possible, to wear the flowers were gathered.

5. It's considered bad luck to give a lei to a pregnant woman. This is because the lei is thought to resemble the umbilical cord, which could wrap around the woman's neck.

Today, Lei Day is celebrated on May 1st each year. The day honors the customs, traditions, and making of leis. The holiday, which continues into the 2nd of May each year, is celebrated throughout the entire state. Each of the Hawaiian Islands has its own lei that's used for the celebration every year.

Hawaii is the Only State with a Second Official Language

Did you know that prior to the arrival of Captain James Cook, the only language that was ever spoken in the islands was Hawaiian? It wasn't until Christian Missionaries came to the island to try to eradicate the Hawaiian religion that English began to be spoken. The missionaries taught the Hawaiian natives how to speak and read English so that they could understand the Bible. That being said, many Hawaiians continued to speak their native language.

For tourists and non-natives, Hawaiian is a complex language. This is because the Hawaiian alphabet is made up of only 12 letters, along with two symbols ('okina and kahakō) that change the sound of a word. This results in many long words, such as Hawaii's state fish: Humuhumunukunukuapua'a. It can take non-natives a lot of practice to learn to pronounce Hawaiian words.

Today, Hawaii is the only state that has a second official language. It wasn't always that way, however. The Hawaiian language was actually banned when the islands became a U.S. territory. It wasn't until 1978 that Hawaiian became an official language.

Sadly, there has been a decrease in the Hawaiian language. It's considered critically endangered. As of 2001, less than 0.1% of the state's population spoke the language.

Aside from English and Hawaiian, three other languages are spoken in the state. These languages are Pidgin (Hawaiian Creole), Samoan, and Tongan. Since Pidgin is commonly spoken throughout the state, many people assume that it's a third official language, but this isn't true. It's often referred to as Hawaii's "unofficial third language," however.

The State of Hawaii is Constantly Growing

Did you know it's possible for a state to grow geographically bigger? Well, it is! The state of Hawaii has continued to grow in size. In fact, it grows an average of 42 acres each year.

Ironically, it's the Big Island of Hawaii that just keeps getting bigger. Between the years of 1983 and 2002, the Big Island of Hawaii grew 543 acres. This is due to volcanic eruptions from Kilauea Volcano, which causes lava and ash to flow into the ocean. Once the lava cools, it forms new land. The volcano has been erupting for more than 30 years.

Everyone in Hawaii is a Minority, Including Caucasians

You may have heard that Hawaii is a "melting pot," but do you know just how much of one it is? Did you know that Hawaii is the only state in the United States where racial or ethnic minorities don't exist? Hawaii is also the only state where Caucasians are a minority! In fact, *everyone* who lives in the state of Hawaii is a minority.

It's been estimated that Caucasians account for approximately 34% of the total Hawaiian population, making it the lowest population of white Americans in the entire United States. The rest of Hawaii's population is made up of Japanese-American (32%), Filipino-American (16%), and Chinese-American (5%).

Hawaii has been found to have the highest number of both Asian-Americans and multicultural Americans in the entire country!

One of the Biggest Tragedies in U.S. History Happened in Hawaii

One of the biggest tragedies in the United States, as well as the worst naval disaster in American history, took place in Hawaii. On Sunday, December 7th, 1941, Pearl Harbor, which is located on the island of Oahu, was attacked by the Japanese at 7:48 a.m. The attack was unannounced in order to catch soldiers off-guard.

The famous quote by then President Franklin Roosevelt, "Yesterday, December 7th, 1941... a date that will live in infamy," was a result of the attack.

The attack on Pearl Harbor is what led to the United States' involvement in the war. The next day, the United States announced that they were declaring war on Japan.

The attack resulted in the loss of 2,335 American soldiers. An addition 1,143 soldiers were also wounded during the attack. In total, 18 ships were run aground, including five battleships.

Hawaii Was the First State to Legalize Abortion

Did you know that Hawaii was the first state to ever legalize abortion on the request of the woman?

Abortions requested by women became legal in the state in 1970. There were some limitations: the woman had to reside in the state for 90 days prior to the abortion and the abortion had to be performed before 20 weeks of pregnancy. New York was the next state to follow suit.

Hawaii made abortion legal prior to Roe vs. Wade, which happened in 1971.

A Former President of the United States is From Hawaii

One United States President was born in Hawaii. If you know anything about American politics, then you probably already know that it's Barack Obama!

Barack Obama was born at the Kapiolani Medical Center for Women and Children, which is located in Honolulu.

While Obama was born in Honolulu, he didn't spend his entire childhood in the state. In fact, a few weeks after Barack was born, his parents moved to Seattle, Washington where his father attended the University of Washington.

A year later, the family moved back to Hawaii where Barack's father attended graduate school at the University of Hawaii on a scholarship.

Obama's father moved back to his home country of Kenya in 1964.

When Barack was six years old, he and his mother moved to Indonesia with his stepfather. Barack

Obama attended school in Indonesia until he was 10 years old.

In 1971, Barack returned to Hawaii where he lived with his maternal grandparents. Obama attended Punahou School, a private college prep school. He graduated from Punahou School in 1979.

Obama has said that experiencing Hawaii's various cultures while growing up helped shape his world views and values.

While growing up in Hawaii, Barack went by the nickname "Barry," which remained with him during the course of his presidency.

Not only is Obama the only former U.S. President who was born in Hawaii, but he's also the only former POTUS who was born outside of the 48 contiguous states!

There Are No Snakes in Hawaii

If you're afraid of snakes, then you might want to consider relocating to Hawaii. There are no snakes that are native to Hawaii, aside from the Brahminy blind snake, which was imported from the Philippines. The Brahminy blind snake is about the size of an earthworm and completely harmless. Otherwise, no snakes can be found in the state and you're banned from having them. In fact, it's actually a *crime* to bring a snake to the state!

It's considered a Class C felony to transport or own snakes in Hawaii, which carries a sentence of up to three years in prison and a $200,000 fine. This might seem like a strange law for a state to have, but there is a good reason behind it. Snakes are banned in the state because snakes eat eggs, which poses a threat to Hawaii's endangered bird species.

Snakes aren't the only animal that's banned in Hawaii. Alligators, dragon lizards, geckos, piranhas, snapping turtles, toucans, hamsters, ferrets, and gerbils are also banned in the state.

RANDOM FACTS

1. The state of Hawaii encompasses 6,422 square miles. The Big Island takes up 4,028 square miles or approximately 63% of the total land mass in the state. The Big Island is double the size of Hawaii's other islands combined. The Big Island of Hawaii also encompasses more square miles than Delaware and Rhode Island combined.

2. Hawaii is the most isolated place in the world. It's approximately 2,390 miles away from California, 3,850 miles away from Japan, 4,900 miles away from China, and 5,280 miles away from the Philippines. Honolulu is the most remote city in the United States.

3. Honolulu is the largest city in the entire world. This is because any island not named as belonging to a county belongs to Honolulu, as per the Hawaii State Constitution. This means Oahu, which Honolulu is located on, and many other small islands are all part of Honolulu. Honolulu is about 1,500 miles long. To put this into perspective, it would stretch from Los Angeles, California to Denver, Colorado. (Bonus fact: the word *Honolulu* means "sheltered harbor" in the Hawaiian language).

4. The total population of Hawaii is estimated to be around 1.4 million, making it the 40th most populous state in the U.S. The island of Oahu, however, is home to an estimated 983,429 people as of 2013. This makes the island more populated than six states, individually. Oahu has a higher population than Alaska, Delaware, North Dakota, South Dakota, Vermont, and Wyoming.

5. The first Asian-American to ever be elected to the United States Senate was from Hawaii. Hiram Fong was born in Honolulu to Chinese immigrant parents. In 1959, he became the first Asian-American and the first Chinese-American to ever be elected as a state Senator.

6. Research has found that living in paradise might help you live longer. Hawaiians have the highest average life expectancy in America. It's been estimated that Hawaiians live an average of six years longer than Mississippians, who have the lowest average life expectancy. Studies have found that Hawaiians live an average of 82.4 years, which is 3.7 years longer than the contiguous United States national average of 78.7, according to an article published in the *Hawai'i Journal of Medicine and Public Health* in January of 2017.

7. Hawaii does not observe Daylight Saving Time. It also has a time zone of its own, which is called

Hawaiian Standard Time. The reason for this is due to where Hawaii is situated geographically. Since Hawaii is further south from the other U.S. states, there's no advantage to the state observing Daylight Saving Time. With the state's close proximity to the equator, the timing of sunrises and sunsets doesn't vary as much as it does in the north. Hawaii isn't the only state that doesn't observe Daylight Saving Time. Most of the state of Arizona doesn't take part in it, either.

8. In ancient Hawaii, the natives lived by rules or prohibitions. These rules were known as *kapu,* which means "forbidden" in the Hawaiian language. During those times the *maka'ainana* (or common people) couldn't allow their shadows to touch the shadow of the Ali'i (or noble people). Women weren't allowed to eat with men or consume certain foods (including bananas, coconut, pork, and certain types of fish). Women also weren't allowed to cook or eat taro. The reason women weren't allowed to eat certain foods is that the foods were reserved for the Ali'i or were saved for the gods. Breaking kapu often resulted in death. Queen Kaahumanu under the Kamehameha Dynasty eliminated many of these prohibitions.

9. When the Europeans arrived in Hawaii, they brought disease with them that caused devastating effects to the native Hawaiian population. It's been

estimated that Hawaii's native population decreased from 300,000 in the 1770s to 60,000 in the 1850s. By 1920, only an estimated 24,000 native Hawaiians remained. It wasn't until Asians began to settle on the islands towards the end of the 19th century that population in the region began to recover.

10. Like every other state, Hawaii has a number of strange laws. If you live in the state, you're subject to being fined if you don't own a boat. You cannot legally have more than one alcoholic beverage in front of you at one time. It's illegal to put coins in your ears. It's against the law to annoy birds in state parks. Dynamite, poison, and electric currents cannot legally be used for fishing purposes. You can't have more than 15 cats and dogs in one home. It's illegal to ride in the back seat of a car without wearing a seatbelt, *but* it's okay to ride in the bed of a truck (without taking any safety measures) if all seats in the vehicle are occupied.

11. Luaus (or traditional Hawaiian parties, which include entertainment) commonly take place in Hawaii. Most children's first birthdays take place in the form of a luau. Wedding and graduations are also often frequently celebrated with luaus.

12. Hawaii is one of the only states in the country that's antipodal (or diametrically opposite on the other side of the globe). This means that the

islands of Hawaii and Oahu are located exactly opposite of Africa's Botswana and Namibia. If you were to dig a hole through Honolulu and to the other side of the globe, you would end up in Botswana or Namibia.

13. There are only four counties throughout all of Hawaii. They are Kauai, Honolulu County, Maui, and Hawaii. There are a mayor and council that serves in each county.

14. Iolani Palace was lit up with electricity four years before the White House was. This happened because King Kalakaua, who had a fascination with technology, traveled to the International Exposition in Paris. It was there that he met Thomas Edison, who had just filed for a patent for the light bulb in the United States. This sparked the King's interest in bringing electricity to Honolulu. Five years later, in 1886, King Kalakaua had electricity installed in the Iolani Palace. Lamps were lit to honor the King's 50th birthday. The Iolani Palace was also the first palace in the entire world that had flushable toilets.

15. Only people who have native Hawaiian ancestry identify themselves as "Hawaiians." People who were born and raised in the state refer to themselves as "locals." Referring to yourself as "Hawaiian" when you were only born in the state is considered disrespectful to the natives.

16. King Kamehameha Day is celebrated on June 11th every year in Hawaii. Parades and festivals take place during the holiday. Unsurprisingly, Hawaii is the only state in the U.S. that has a holiday to honor a monarch.

17. Hawaii is one of only two states in the country that have made gambling illegal. (The other state is Utah). Casinos and slot machines can't be found in the state. It's illegal to play poker or any other card games that involve betting. The law also includes horse races, sports betting, lotteries, and even playing Bingo for money! You also can't make any bets on ships in the state.

18. The Hawaiian flag's design consists of eight horizontal stripes. Each stripe represents one of the eight main islands. There's also a small version of the British flag at the top left-hand corner. This is in honor of George Vancouver, who gave Hawaii its first flag back in 1794.

19. Waikiki Beach is one of Hawaii's most popular destinations. During the 19th century, Hawaiian royals spent a lot of time at Waikiki Beach. The beach is actually made up of five separate beaches: Waikiki, Gray's, Kuhio, Fort DeRussy, and Duke Kahanamoku. With its beautiful white sands and blue waters, Waikiki is responsible for about $2 billion or about 42% of Hawaii's tourism industry revenue. It draws in an average of

72,000 tourists every day or about 50% of Hawaii's tourists. In Hawaiian, the word *Waikiki* means "spouting waters."

20. Hawaii is the only state in the U.S. that's located in Oceania. Oceania is a geographic region which also includes Polynesia, Australia, New Zealand, New Guinea, and other islands.

Test Yourself – Questions and Answers

1. The first European to discover the Hawaii Islands was:

   a. Captain James Hook
   b. Captain James Cook
   c. George Vancouver

2. Hawaii is made up of how many islands?

   a. 8
   b. 32
   c. 132

3. The island that once served as a leper colony was:

   a. Molokai
   b. Oahu
   c. Kauai

4. Hawaii was the first state to ever legalize:

   a. abortion
   b. gay marriage
   c. guns

5. Research has found that Hawaiians have an average life expectancy of:

   a. 92.4 years
   b. 82.4 years
   c. 82.7 years

Answers

1. b.
2. c.
3. a.
4. a.
5. b.

CHAPTER TWO

HAWAII'S MAIN ISLANDS AND OTHER FACTS ABOUT THE STATE

Hawaii's islands were formed by undersea volcanoes, which erupted thousands—or even millions—of years ago. How much do you know about the state's main islands? Do you know who the island of Maui is named after? Do you know the state's official nicknames? Do you know which flowers and colors are traditionally used when lei-making on each island? Do you know which rare marsupial can be spotted on one of Hawaii's islands? To learn the answers to these and other facts about Hawaii's main islands, read on!

Hawaii's Main Islands Have Nicknames

It may be known as the Aloha State, but did you know that Hawaii's eight main islands have nicknames?

The Big Island (of Hawaii)

The island of Hawaii is known as "The Big Island" or "Big Island of Hawaii." This because it's—you guessed it—the biggest of the eight main islands.

The Gathering Place

Oahu is called "The Gathering Place." This is because 80% of Hawaii's population lives on the island. It's regarded as the main island. It's also the island that sees the most tourists. In fact, Oahu gets more tourists than every other Hawaiian island *combined*. In 2016, the island saw more than 8.94 million visitors.

The Valley Isle

Maui is nicknamed "The Valley Isle." This is because of the large valley located between the northwestern and southeastern volcanoes on the island.

The Garden Isle

Kauai is called "The Garden Isle." It earned this nickname because the majority of the island's land consists of rainforests and mountain ranges. Kauai is also known as the "wettest spot on earth," with its annual average rainfall reaching 460 inches.

The Pineapple Isle

Lanai is known as "The Pineapple Isle." Although pineapples are produced on all of Hawaii's islands,

Lanai was once responsible for producing 3/4 of the world's pineapples.

The Target Isle

The island of Kahoolawe is nicknamed "The Target Isle" (and no, it has nothing to do with the department store). This nickname was given to the island because it was used by the U.S. Army as a training ground during WWII. The public is forbidden from visiting the island since there might still be bombs that have yet to explode.

The Forbidden Isle

Even though Kahoolawe is off-limits to the public, the nickname of "The Forbidden Isle" goes to another island: Niihau. This is because the island is privately owned. Elizabeth Sinclair bought it from King Kamehameha V back in 1864 for $10,000. It's currently owned by her descendants, the Robinson family. Aside from the owners, only government officials and the U.S. Navy are permitted to use the island.

The Friendly Isle

Molokai is nicknamed "The Friendly Isle." Molokai is home to the highest amount of people with native Hawaiian ancestry. The island is the least touristy, most laidback, and "friendliest" of all the accessible islands.

The Ages of the Islands

Have you ever wondered which of Hawaii's islands is the youngest? It might surprise you to learn that while the Big Island of Hawaii is the biggest island in the state, it's also the youngest. The Big Island is less than 500,000 years old.

So, which of Hawaii's islands is the oldest? That would be Kauai, which has been around for approximately 5 million years!

From oldest to youngest, the islands' ages are believed to be as follows:

1. Kauai – 5 million years
2. Niihau – 4.9 million years
3. Oahu – 2.2 to 3.4 million years
4. Molokai – 1.3 and 1.9 million years
5. Lanai – 1.3 million years
6. Maui – 800,000 to 1.3 million years
7. Kahoolawe – 1 million years
8. The Big Island of Hawaii – 500,000 years

The Islands and Their Sizes

You already know that the Big Island is the largest of Hawaii's islands, but do you know just *how* big it is? Do you know which of Hawaii's islands is the smallest? Let's take a closer look at the Hawaiian Islands from largest to smallest.

1. **Hawaii (The Big Island)** – At 4,028 square miles, the island of Hawaii is the largest island

in both Hawaii *and* the United States.

2. **Maui** – Spanning across 727.7 square miles, Maui is the second largest of the Hawaiian Islands.

3. **Oahu** – Encompassing 596.7 square miles, the most popular island among tourists is the third largest island in Hawaii.

4. **Kauai** – With a total of 562.3 square miles, Kauai is the fourth largest island.

5. **Molokai** – At 260 square miles, Molokai is the fifth largest Hawaiian island.

6. **Lanai** – Taking up a total of 140.5 square miles, Lanai is the smallest publicly accessible of Hawaii's islands.

7. **Niihau** – Spanning across 69.5 square miles, the privately-owned Niihau island is Hawaii's second smallest.

8. **Kahoolawe** – With just 44.59 square miles, Kahoolawe is the smallest Hawaiian main island.

The Big Island is Home to Some Record-Breaking Volcanoes

Did you know that Hawaii is home to one of the largest volcanoes on Earth? That volcano would be Mauna Loa, which is located on the Big Island of Hawaii.

For many years, Mauna Loa was considered to be the largest volcano on Earth. That all changed in 2013, however, when Tamu Massif was recognized as Earth's largest volcano.

Mauna Loa, whose name means "long mountain," has an estimated volume of about 18,000 cubic miles.

It's been estimated that Mauna Loa has been erupting for 700,000 years, at least. It's also believed that it emerged above sea level around 400,000 years ago.

The eruptions from Mauna Loa are generally non-explosive and very fluid. Eruptions that took place in 1926 and 1950 destroyed entire villages. The city of Hilo is built on lava flows.

The Hawaiian Volcano Observatory has been monitoring the volcano since 1912.

It has been predicted that Mauna Loa won't always be where it is right now. Scientists say that the slow drift of the Pacific Plate is eventually going to carry the volcano away within the next 500,000 to one million years. This will cause the volcano to become extinct.

While Mauna Loa may be the 2nd largest volcano on Earth, it's not the most active. The volcano hasn't erupted in recent years, with the last eruption taking place in 1984.

Kīlauea is the most active of the five volcanoes that can be found on the Big Island. The volcano erupted 61 times since 1823 and has continuously erupted since 1983, making it one of the most active volcanoes on Earth.

The name "Kīlauea" means "spreading, much spewing." It is the youngest of Hawaii's volcanoes. It's believed to be between 300,000 and 600,000 years old and is thought to only have emerged from sea level around 100,00 years ago. The volcano has been responsible for much destruction over the course of its lifetime. It destroyed the town of Kalapana in 1990 and Vacationland Hawaii in 2018. In 2018, the eruption was coupled with a strong earthquake, leading to a major evacuation.

While Mauna Loa and Kīlauea are the most notable volcanoes that can be found on the Big Island of Hawaii, there are three more:

1. Hualālai is the third youngest and third most active volcano on the island. Its last eruption took place in 1801.
2. Mauna Kea is a dormant volcano, but still holds a couple of records. Its 13,802-foot peak makes it the highest point in Hawaii and the second-highest point above sea level of any island on Earth.
3. Kohala, which is estimated to be one million years old, is the oldest of Hawaii's volcanoes. It is considered extinct, as it hasn't experienced any lava flows for 4,500 years.

If you want to get a closer look at Hawaii's volcanoes, then you're in luck. Hawai'i Volcanoes National Park lets you see Mauna Loa and Kīlauea up close and personal. The park sees more than 2.5 million visitors each year.

Hawaii's Beaches Come in a Variety of Colors

When you think of Hawaii, you probably think of beautiful beige or white sand beaches—the type of beaches straight out of a postcard or honeymoon brochure. Not all of Hawaii's beaches have white sand, though! There are a number of other sand colors that can be found throughout the Aloha State.

Red sand beaches are incredibly rare. In fact, there are only a few red sand beaches throughout the entire world—and one of the most famous ones just so happens to be located in Maui. Kaihalulu Beach, which is located on Maui's eastern coast, is a sight to see.

Black sand beaches are common throughout the state of Hawaii. One of the most famous black sand beaches in the state is Punaluu Beach, located on the Big Island of Hawaii. Wainapanapa Beach in Maui is another one of the state's most popular black sand beaches. The sand at Wainapanapa is made up of smooth lava pebbles.

There are only four green sand beaches in the entire

world and one of them can be found in the Aloha State! Papakolea Beach, which is located on the Big Island of Hawaii, gets its green sand from olivine, a mineral that's produced by Hawaii's volcanic lava.

At Papohaku Beach in Molokai, you'll find orange sand. It takes on more of a yellow color during the day, but it looks very orange when the sun sets!

Though Kailua Beach in Oahu is a white sand beach, it's well-known for its beauty. The island's most visited beach has sand that's made up of coral, seashell fragments, and other materials.

And if you're wondering which island has the most beaches, that would be Maui. Maui has 80 beaches that span 30 miles. The island's beaches are more accessible than any other island in Hawaii.

The Most Dangerous Beach in the State Can Be Found in Oahu

When you think of Hawaii, you might not consider that one of its beaches could be dangerous. But one of the 125 beaches in Oahu is the most dangerous beach in the Aloha State.

Sandy Beach Park is one of the most popular beaches in the state for experienced surfers and bodyboarders. When it comes to swimming, however, amateurs should avoid its water. The beach is known for its powerful waves and shore break. Even when the waves appear to be calm, there are also dangerous currents.

Sadly, Sandy Beach Park has been nicknamed "Broke Neck Beach." This is because many people have become paralyzed due to the beach's notorious spine-altering waves. A number of drownings have also taken place at the beach.

Rumor has it that there's an ambulance permanently stationed in the beach's parking lot.

While there are many other beaches throughout the state that pose equal dangers to inexperienced surfers or swimmers, Sandy Beach Park is, by far, the most dangerous.

Hawaii's Islands Are Represented by Colors and Flowers

Did you know that each of Hawaii's islands has an official color and flower? They were chosen by the state back in 2000. Although most leis are made from plumeria and tuberose, carnations, and orchids, each island is known for making leis out of its signature flowers and colors, which are generally the flowers most commonly found on the island.

These flowers and colors have been officially chosen to represent each state:

1. **The Big Island (Hawaii)** – The official color of the Big Island is red. The color red is thought

to represent the fire goddess, who spills her lava along the island shores and into the sea. The pua lehua, or Ohia, flower represents the island. The red flowers, which have feathery blossoms, also come in shades of orange and yellow.

2. **Oahu** – The island of Oahu's official color is yellow, while the puailima (ilima) flower is the official island flower. Although ilima flowers come in orange and red, the yellow ilima is the most common. The ilima flower is considered to be a symbol of love.

3. **Maui** – The color pink was chosen to represent the island of Maui because the lokelani or Maui rose can be found throughout the island. It's the only official island flower that isn't actually native to Hawaii. The lokelani was brought from Asia back in the 1800s. The flower, which is bright pink in color, is known for its fragrance.

4. **Kauai** – The official color of Kauai is purple. It was chosen due to the purple flowers of the Mokihana, the official island flower. The purple flowers, as well as the green berries also produced by the trees, are commonly used in Kauai leis.

5. **Molokai** – Green is the color that was chosen to represent Molokai. The color was chosen because Molokai is mostly rural. The white

kukui blossom, which comes from the pua kukui tree, is the official island flower. The tiny white flowers are found in clusters. Leis are made from the blossoms, as well as kukui nuts, which come in both spotted brown and black varieties. The pua kukui is also Hawaii's official state tree.

6. **Lanai** – Orange is the official color of Lanai. This is a good representation of the island, which tends to be drier than the other islands due to less rainfall. The island flower is the kaunaoa, which is also known as the native dodder. The ground-hugging plant is light orange and white.

7. **Niihau** – The official color of Hawaii's privately-owned island is white. While visitors aren't prohibited to visit "The Forbidden Island," leis from Niihau are highly prized. While the island doesn't have an official flower like the others, it *does* have an official lei-making material: pupu shells. The leis are often made from white pupu shells. Other shell colors include pinks, tans, and peaches.

8. **Kahoolawe** – This island, which has no residents and doesn't allow visitors, is represented by the color of gray. The hinahina plant, which is found on the island, has leaves with tiny hairs that give off a gray or silver appearance.

How the Main Islands Got Their Names

In Chapter One, we talked about how Hawaii may have gotten its name. But do you know where the other seven main islands got their names?

1. **Oahu** – The word "O'ahu" (or Oahu) doesn't have a meaning in the Hawaiian language. It has been said that Hawaii Loa, the legendary Polynesian who may have discovered the Hawaiian Islands, named the island after one of his sons.

2. **Maui** – The island of Maui was named after the demigod of the same name. According to Hawaiian lore, the shape of the island resembles Maui's body and head. Legend says that Maui invented a giant fishhook from his dead grandmother's jawbone. Lore says that when Maui used the hook to fish, he lifted the Hawaiian Islands up from the sea and lassoed the sun onto the volcano Haleakala. Maui also allegedly invented spears and taught Hawaiians how to build fires.

3. **Molokai** – There are several theories on how the island got its name. Some say it means "rough water" or "spinning water." Others say that the island may have been named after a chief in ancient times.

4. **Kauai** – Though the meaning of "Kauai" is a bit of a mystery, it has been said that the

meaning of Kauai may be "a favorite place around one's neck." The meaning allegedly comes from the legendary Hawaii Loa, whose favorite son may have been named Kauai. "A favorite place around one's neck" is thought to be the best place to carry one's most beloved child.

5. **Lanai** – While no one knows for sure where the name "Lanai" came from, it's believed to originate from "Lānaʻi o Kauluāʻau," which means "day of the conquest of Kauluāʻau" or "triumphant day." This is a reference to an old legend about a prince named Kauluāʻau from Maui. Kauluāʻau was banished to Lanai after causing mischief at his father's palace in the town of Lahaina. The island of Lanai was allegedly haunted by ghosts and goblins. Kauluāʻau was able to chase them away, restoring peace to the island and winning his father's approval again.

6. **Niihau** – It's unclear where "Niihau" came from, but it's thought it might originate from the Chinese word "ni hao." *Ni hao* means "hello."

7. **Kahoolawe** – The word *Kahoolawe* translates to "the carrying away (by currents)."

One of Lanai's Most Popular Attractions is Thought to be Otherworldly

Did you know that one of the most popular attractions on the island of Lanai is believed to be otherworldly?

Keahiakawelo, which is most commonly known as "The Garden of the Gods" or "The Fires of Kawelo," is a popular tourist attraction on the island of Lanai. It's a red lava formation that's located in the northern part of Lanai. There are a couple of legends about how the garden was formed.

According to one Hawaiian lore, the Garden of the Gods was formed by gods who threw rocks from the sky while tending to their gardens.

Another Hawaiian legend says that two kahunas (or priests) from the islands of Lanai and Molokai had a contest to keep a fire burning on their islands longer than the other. The prize would be that the winning island would be rewarded with great abundance. Kawelo, who was the kahuna of Lanai, is said to have used all of the vegetation in Keahiakawelo in order to keep his fire burning. It's believed that's why the area is so barren today.

Regardless of how the Garden of the Gods was formed, it has been said that the best time to visit is when the sun sets. At that time of day, the sunlight casts a glow over the lava rocks, giving them a red or purple appearance.

The World's Largest Dormant Volcano is Located in Maui

Did you know that there are no active volcanoes on the island of Maui? In fact, only three volcanoes in the state are considered to be active and all of those are located on the Big Island of Hawaii.

That being said, the largest dormant volcano in the entire world can be found on the island of Maui. The volcano is Haleakala, which spans 21 miles in length, 2 miles in width, and 2,600 feet in depth. The volcano is so large that the entire island of Manhattan could fit inside the volcano! Also known as the East Maui Volcano, Haleakala is a shield volcano that forms over 75% of Maui.

It's believed that Haleakala last erupted sometime between 1480 and 1600. Additionally, the volcano has only erupted three times in the last 900 years.

The Largest Ranch in the U.S. is Located on the Big Island

Did you know that the largest ranch in the United States is located on the Big Island of Hawaii?

Encompassing 480,000 acres, the Parker Ranch is the largest cattle ranch in the country. Founded by John Palmer Parker in 1847, the Parker Ranch is also one of the oldest ranches in the U.S.

The land was given to Parker by Kamehameha I. Parker helped Kamehameha I get rid of feral bulls on the island of Hawaii. In exchange, Kamehameha gave him the land.

The ranch plays an important role in Hawaii's history. The Parker family and Hawaiian royals had ties as both rulers and friends. Through conflicts and changes over the years, the Parkers and Hawaiian royals maintained their positive relationship.

Today, Parker Ranch lives on through a charitable trust.

Bonus fact: Have you ever wondered what to call a cowboy on a ranch in Hawaii? Cowboys are called *paniolo.* "Paniolo" is a Hawaiian pronunciation of a Spanish word. The first cowboys spoke Spanish and migrated from California. In Hawaiian, there is no "s" sound.

Oahu is Home to This Rare Marsupial

Did you know that Hawaii is home to wallabies? While the marsupial is native to Australia, there are brush-tailed rock wallabies on the island of Oahu.

Wondering how they got there in the first place? Rumor has it that two wallabies escaped from a private Hawaii zoo. This is allegedly what led to the population of wallabies on Oahu.

The wallabies, which weigh 10 to 15 pounds, used to

live between Nuuanu to Halawa Valley. Today, however, it's believed that there's just one small colony left in Kalihi Valley.

Sightings of Oahu's wallabies occur so infrequently that many people don't even believe the elusive animals exist on the island at all. There hadn't been an official sighting since the 1990s, though people claimed to still see the tiny marsupials. Some people thought the wallabies were nothing more than an urban legend, but there was a sighting at Halawa Correctional Facility in February of 2018.

One retired state wildlife manager believes there are approximately 40 wallabies left on Oahu.

It's illegal to hunt the state's wallabies since they are considered a threatened species in Australia.

You Can Take the "Drive of a Lifetime" on Maui

Did you know the Hana Highway in Maui has been named a "Drive of a Lifetime" by *National Geographic*? And for good reason. The Hana Highway, which spans more than 60 miles, is home to 59 bridges and 620 curves. During the drive, you'll come across waterfalls, seascapes, and more as you drive through a tropical rainforest.

Mark Zuckerberg Owns an Estate on Kauai

Did you know that Facebook CEO Mark Zuckerberg owns an estate on Kauai?

The social media site's co-founder purchased 700 acres of waterfront land on the island. He and his wife paid $100 million for their estate.

In 2017, Zuckerberg stirred up some controversy among the locals when he filed lawsuits against hundreds of Kauai natives. Natives own the land that falls on Zuckerberg's estate. In a move that was intended to buy his privacy, Zuckerberg tried to sue for "quiet title and partition," a legal action which would have forced the property owners to sell the land to the highest bidder. It's an action that's taken to settle who Hawaii land belongs to, as it's often unclear.

This was the case in Zuckerberg's lawsuit. The property he was trying to obtain crossed many generations and heirs. Some of the legal agreements for the land dates back over 160 years.

Zuckerberg's legal action outraged many Hawaiian citizens. Some felt that the Facebook CEO was the "face of neocolonialism," according to *The Guardian*. As with other native cultures, having a claim to the land is important to Hawaiian natives. Other people in Hawaii felt the action was unnecessary and unneighbourly, especially after Zuckerberg claimed he had a deep respect for the Hawaiian native culture and values.

After stirring up so much controversy and realizing the law is different in Hawaii than in the other 49 states, Zuckerberg dropped the lawsuit.

Humpback Whales Are Most Seen off This Island

If you love whale-watching, then you probably already know that Hawaii is a great place to see humpback whales.

Hawaii is considered to be the 3rd best spot to go whale-watching in the entire world. It's been estimated that anywhere from 10,000 to 18,000 humpback whales make their way to the islands every year. They travel 3,500 miles from Alaska to Hawaii where they breed, give birth, and nurse their young. They live there during the winter and spring months before journeying back to Alaska.

There are a number of good places to see humpback whales in the Aloha State. The Big Island is considered to be the best place to see humpback whales, with the Kohala Coast having the greatest number of whales. Humpback whales can also be spotted from Maui and Kauai. There's a ferry that takes visitors from the channel between Maui and Molokai, where you can spot many humpback whales.

Known as *na kohola* in the Hawaiian language, humpback whales are believed to play a big role in Hawaiian culture. Humpback whales, which are approximately 45-feet long, are thought to represent the Hawaiian god Kanaloa. Kanaloa is the god of ocean animals.

While humpback whales can be seen in Hawaii any time between November and May, the best time to see them is between January and March. Humpback whales are also seen most frequently during the early morning hours. There are also whale-watching tours throughout the state.

RANDOM FACTS

1. The Hawaiian Islands span across 1,523 miles in total. This means the islands of Hawaii are the longest island chain in the entire world!

2. The reef off of Kumimi Beach on the island of Molokai is America's longest continuous fringing reef. This makes Molokai one of the top places to go snorkeling in the world.

3. The amount of rainfall in Maui widely varies. Lahaina only gets about 10 inches of rainfall per year, while Pu'u Kukui experiences an annual average of 365 inches of rain.

4. Ka Lae, which is located on the Big Island, is the southernmost point in the U.S.

5. Oahu is said to have the second worst traffic in the entire United States. (No. 1 is Los Angeles, California). Traffic is mostly found on the freeways near Honolulu and tends to be most problematic during the Triple Crown of Surfing.

6. The island of Molokai is home to some of the tallest sea cliffs in the entire world. Some of the island's sea cliffs are over 3,000 feet tall.

7. Astronauts completed their training in Hawaii during the 1960s. This is because the Big Island's

hardened lava fields from the volcano Mauna Loa are very similar to the surface of the moon.

8. Hawaii is one of the only places in the world that has two different types of lava. It's home to both a'a (rough, rocky, fragmented lava) and pahoehoe (smooth lava).

9. The island of Molokai doesn't have any traffic lights. This is because there is so little traffic on the island that a traffic light isn't needed.

10. Hawaii only has two native animal species: the monk seal and the hoary bat. The monk seal is one of the rarest marine mammals in the world. There are less than 1,200 monk seals left in the wild, making them a critically endangered species. You can get a fine if you "harass" a monk seal in Hawaii.

11. It's illegal for buildings in Kauai to be built higher than palm trees.

12. *Conde Nast Traveler* magazine has voted Maui the "Best Island in the World" sixteen times!

13. The last royal coconut grove in Hawaii can be found on Molokai. Kapuaiwa Coconut Grove boasts itself as "one of the last royal coconut groves in the state." The coconut grove was allegedly planted for King Kamehameha V.

14. Kauai is home to the largest protected population of Hawaii's state bird, the nene goose. You can

also expect to see Kauai's unofficial bird: the chicken. Chickens run free on the island ever since many of the farmers' chicken coops were destroyed during Hurricane Iniki back in 1992.

15. You can mail a coconut instead of a postcard from Hawaii. Post offices throughout the state allow you to choose a coconut for free, which you can decorate, write an address on, and then place stamps on before mailing it to someone.

16. Thanks to the Kilauea volcano, vog is common in Hawaii. Vog is volcanic haze that's generally harmless, but it can cause issues for people who have asthma or respiratory problems. The vog magnifies the sun and moon, giving them a larger-than-usual, orange appearance. This leads to beautiful sunsets.

17. Between all of its islands, Hawaii has 11 out of the 13 climate zones. It's home to everything from tropical rainforests to deserts.

18. Banyan Tree Park in Lahaina, Maui is a popular tourist attraction. The tree, which is over 60 feet tall, is the size of an entire city block. It takes up nearly a whole acre. The Banyan is a popular spot for events and activities to be held.

19. The island of Oahu consists of two mountain ranges. The Waianae Range in West Oahu is approximately 3.9 million years old, while the

Ko'olau Range is estimated to only be 2.7 million years old.

20. While Hawaii is most well-known for its beautiful weather, it does snow in the state. It doesn't snow much, however. The only place in the state where there's snow on a yearly basis is Mauna Kea. It also sometimes snows at Haleakala on Maui.

Test Yourself – Questions and Answers

1. The Hawaiian island that's named after a demigod is

   a. Oahu
   b. Kauai
   c. Maui

2. The largest volcano on Earth, which is located on the Big Island, is:

   a. Kīlauea
   b. Mauna Loa
   c. Hualālai

3. The world's largest dormant volcano is located on:

   a. Maui
   b. Oahu
   c. The Big Island

4. The tallest sea cliffs in the world can be found on which of Hawaii's islands?

   a. Niihau
   b. Molokai
   c. Kauai

5. Astronauts in the 1960s completed their training on which Hawaiian island?

   a. Kauai
   b. Niihau
   c. The Big Island

Answers

1. c.
2. b.
3. a.
4. b.
5. c.

CHAPTER THREE

HAWAII'S POPCULTURE AND SPORTS

Have you ever wondered what movies were filmed in Hawaii? Do you know which famous movie's fictional waterfalls are actually in Hawaii? Do you know which actress got her start thanks to a role she landed as an extra in a film that was shot in Hawaii? Do you know which sport was invented in the state? Do you know which inspirational person came from the state? Do you know which famous athletes are from Hawaii? What do you know about professional sports in the Aloha State? Read on to learn more about Hawaii's pop culture!

Bruno Mars Was Raised by a Musical Family in Honolulu

Did you know that music sensation Bruno Mars was born and raised in the Waikiki neighborhood of Honolulu?

Bruno Mars, whose real name is Peter Gene Hernandez, was born to parents with musical backgrounds themselves. His mother was a singer and dancer, while his father played rock and roll music. His parents actually met when they performed in a show together, during which his father played percussion and his mother was a hula dancer.

Peter was one of six children. When Peter was just two years old, his father gave him the nickname "Bruno" because he resembled pro wrestler Bruno Sammartino.

It was while he was living in Honolulu that Bruno Mars' love for music began. His uncle was an Elvis Presley impersonator and encouraged Bruno to begin performing on the stage when he was just three years old. Mars would perform songs by artists like Michael Jackson, the Temptations, and The Isley Brothers.

When Bruno Mars was four years old, he began to perform with The Love Notes, his family's band.

By the time he was five, Bruno Mars was famous on Oahu for his Elvis Presley impersonation. In 1990, Mars was featured in the *MidWeek* tabloid, in which he was referred to as "Little Elvis." He also landed a role in *Honeymoon in Vegas*, starring Nicholas Cage and Sarah Jessica Parker.

Mars' impersonation of Elvis Presley shaped him into the artist he is today.

When he was attending President Theodore Roosevelt High School in Honolulu, Bruno Mars also performed with a group known as The School Boys.

It was after Bruno Mars' sister moved to Los Angeles that his musical career really got started. His sister played Mars' demo for Mike Lynn of Dr. Dre's Aftermath Entertainment. Lynn liked what he heard, and Bruno Mars moved to Los Angeles.

Peter chose his stage name due to the nickname that was given to him by his father. He chose Mars because girls always told him he was "out of this world." He also chose the stage name because the music industry wanted him to sing in Spanish.

The rest is history. Bruno Mars went on to produce and record songs for artists like Adam Levine, Sean Kingston, Flo Rida, and Brandy.

Mars rose to fame when his vocals were featured in the hit songs, "Billionaire" by Travie McCoy and "Nothin' on You" by B.O.B.

Later, Mars' solo songs, "Just the Way You Are," "Grenade," and "The Lazy Song" shot to the top of the charts. He won a Grammy for his song "It Will Rain," which was featured in *The Twilight Saga: Breaking Dawn – Part I.*

From his second album, Bruno Mars' songs "Locked Out of Heaven" and "When I Was Your Man" hit No. 1 on the *Billboard* Hot 100.

And to think, it all started out in Honolulu!

A Disney Animated Film Took Place in Hawaii

The 2002 Disney animated film *Lilo & Stitch* is about a Hawaiian girl named Lilo. Lilo and her older sister were orphaned after their parents died in a car accident. In the film, Lilo meets an extraterrestrial creature, whose name is Experiment 626. Lilo adopts the creature as her "dog," which she names "Stitch."

Stitch has been genetically altered to destroy things and get into mischief. Lilo and Stitch still manage to form a close bond with one another—a bond that leads Stitch to change his ways in order to remain with Lilo.

Lilo & Stitch drew attention to the Hawaiian word *ohana*. The movie defines ohana as "family," but the Hawaiian concept of the word goes much deeper than that. Ohana means "extended family," which may apply to people who are blood-related or adopted family, both literally and figuratively speaking. Lilo and Stitch chose one another, making them "ohana."

This Australian Actress is Actually from Honolulu

While she's often thought of as an Australian actress, she's actually from Honolulu. Can you guess who she is?

One hint: she's married to one of the most famous New Zealand musicians.

Nicole Kidman is most well-known for her roles in movies like *Batman Forever*, *Bewitched*, and *Moulin Rouge!* Her marriage to country singer and New Zealand-born musician Keith Urban, who also resided in Australia at one point.

But did you know that Nicole Kidman isn't actually *from* Australia? Kidman was born to Australian parents when they were temporarily living in Honolulu on student visas. As a result, Nicole Kidman was granted both Australian *and* American citizenship, making her Australian-American.

When she was four years old, her family moved back to Australia, where she attended school. It was also in Australia where Kidman's career got started. But it all began in Honolulu!

Lots of Movies Have Been Filmed in the State

With its beautiful landscape, it should come as no surprise to learn that a number of movies have been filmed in Hawaii! Some of the most popular movies that have been shot in the Aloha State include:

- *50 First Dates* – Starring Drew Barrymore and Adam Sandler, this movie was filmed throughout Oahu. Waimanalo Beach, Kualoa Ranch, Waimea Bay, Sea Life Park, and Waikane

Pier are some of the places that can be spotted throughout the film.

- *Forgetting Sarah Marshall* – This romantic comedy, starring Mila Kunis and Jason Segal, was filmed throughout Oahu. Some film locations include the Turtle Bay Resort and La'ie Point.

- *Hunger Games*: *Catching Fire* – You might be surprised to learn that the cornucopia scene in the film was shot at the Turtle Bay Resort in Oahu.

- *Jurassic Park* and *Jurassic World* – The movie series was filmed in many countries, with some scenes being filmed in Hawaii. Manawaiopuna Falls in Kauai are referred to as "Jurassic Falls" in the film. Kauai's Allerton Garden was featured in the franchise. Kualoa Ranch in Oahu also made an appearance in the film.

- *Pirates of the Caribbean: On Stranger Tides* – Scenes throughout the Disney film were filmed in Hawaii. Some of the places featured in the film include Allerton Garden, Kipu Ranch, Groves Farm, Honopu Arch, and Cocoa Palms Hotel on Kauai.

- *The Descendants* – This movie, starring George Clooney, was shot on Oahu and Kauai. Some of the locations featured in the film include the

Elks Club in Honolulu and Hanalei Bay and Tahiti Nui bar in Kauai.

- *Tropic Thunder* – Although this movie took place in Southeast Asia, it was filmed on the island of Kauai. In fact, it was the largest film production in Kauai history. The film was directed by (and starred) Ben Stiller. It also featured Jack Black and Robert Downey Jr.

These are just some of the many movies that have been filmed throughout the state!

Elvis Presley Starred in a Movie Called *Blue Hawaii*

The King of Rock and Roll starred in a movie called *Blue Hawaii*.

In the movie, Presley plays a guy named Chadwick Gates, an Army veteran who is excited to be back home in Hawaii where he hangs out on the beach, surfs, and spends time with his girlfriend. Chadwick's mom wants him to take over the family fruit business, despite his reluctance.

The movie wasn't received too well. While Elvis Presley good mostly good reviews for his performance in the film, the plot was called bland and most believed it lacked substance.

That being said, the movie helped draw some attention to Hawaii's surf culture.

Scenes from the film were shot throughout Waikiki. There were also scenes from the Hilton Hawaiian Village. The movie actually helped draw attention to the famous hotel, thanks largely to Presley's appearance in the film.

Blue Hawaii was the first—but not the last—movie Elvis Presley starred in that was set and filmed in the state. The next Hawaiian movie he played in was *Girls! Girls! Girls!*

A Movie About the Attack on Pearl Harbor Was Filmed in the State

The 2001 film *Pearl Harbor* focused on the tragedy on Pearl Harbor. The film featured Ben Affleck, Josh Hartnett, and Kate Beckinsale, with Alec Baldwin, Cuba Gooding Jr., and Jon Voight appearing in smaller roles. The movie was centered around the attack on Pearl Harbor, but it was primarily a romantic movie.

While the romance in the movie was reviewed poorly, the film did receive a lot of praise for the attacks being mostly accurate.

It might not surprise you to learn that some of the scenes from *Pearl Harbor* took place in Hawaii. The film was shot at Ford Island and throughout Honolulu. Scenes were also filmed on location at Pearl Harbor.

The producer used Hawaii's naval facilities at the time of filming. Active duty military members, as well as people from the local population, acted as extras while the movie was being filmed.

Something that might surprise you was that the actual ocean was *not* used in the film. The film producers used a stadium-like "bowl" filled with water, which was built in Hawaii. The bowl cost $8 million to create. The bowl is currently used for deep-water fishing tournaments and scuba training.

Scenes from the film were also shot in California, Indiana, Nevada, and England.

One Movie That Takes Place in Hawaii Caused a Lot of Controversies

It may come as no surprise to learn that the movie *Aloha* was set in—and filmed throughout—Hawaii. What you might not know is that the movie caused a lot of controversy among Hawaii locals and throughout the country.

The film featured Bradley Cooper, Rachel McAdams, and Emma Stone. It was Emma Stone being cast as the character of Allison Ng that sparked controversy.

The Media Action Network for Asian Americans accused director/producer Cameron Crowe of "whitewashing" (or casting a white actor/actress in a role that could be better portrayed by someone of a different ethnic background). Emma Stone was cast as a character who is meant to be 25% Chinese and 25% native Hawaiian. Most people felt that Stone's red hair, light eyes, and fair, freckled skin weren't a good fit for the role.

Although Crowe claimed that Emma Stone's character was based on a redheaded Hawaiian local of the same ethnic mix, he apologized for miscasting the actress for the role.

Emma Stone has reportedly said that she regrets allowing herself to be miscast for the role.

A Role as an Extra in a Hawaiian Film Led This Award-Winning Actress to Fame

Today, she's most well-known for her spunky red hair, her amazing voice, and her role as Winifred Sanderson in the Halloween cult classic movie, *Hocus Pocus*. But did you know that Bette Midler started out in Hawaii?

The actress was born in Honolulu where her father worked as a painter at a Navy base and her mother was a seamstress. Midler was named after actress Bette Davis, even though the two names are pronounced differently.

Bette Midler was raised in Aiea area of Honolulu. While she was attending Radford High School in Honolulu, Midler was voted "Most Talkative" and "Most Dramatic."

After high school, Midler went on to study drama at the University of Hawaii at Manoa. The actress left the program after just three semesters, however.

Shortly after dropping out of college, Bette Midler landed her first role as a paid extra in the 1966 movie *Hawaii*. She used the money she earned from the role to move to New York City, where she began to star in Off-Off-Broadway productions and then *Fiddler on the Roof* and *Salvation* on Broadway.

Since then, she's gone on to have a successful career in both singing and acting. Musically, she's most well-known for her hit songs "The Wind Beneath My Wings" and "The Rose."

Over the course of her career, Bette Midler has won three Grammy Awards, four Golden Globe Awards, three Emmy Awards, and two Tony Awards.

And it's all because of that small role she had in the movie *Hawaii*!

Surfing Was Invented in Hawaii

Since Hawaii is known for its surf culture, you might not be surprised to learn that surfing (in the United States) originated from the state.

What might surprise you is that surfing has been around for centuries. Surfing was documented back when Captain James Cook first journeyed to the state in 1778. Surfing played a key role in ancient

Polynesian culture. During those times, chiefs were generally the most skilled surfers and had the best wooden boards they used to ride the waves.

Surfing operated on a class system. The ruling classes had access to the best beaches and boards. The commoners weren't given permission to use the same beaches but proving their ability to surf helped them gain prestige.

Traditionally, surfing wasn't done for entertainment or as an extreme sport or recreational activity the way it is today. In ancient Hawaii, surfing was done as a spiritual pastime and became an important part of native culture. Surfing was also used to train warriors.

The ancient Hawaiians called surfing *he'e nalu*, which translates into "wave sliding."

During those times, the dangers of surfing were acknowledged. The Hawaiians would pray to the gods for protection and strength before they rode the waves into the mysterious ocean. If the ocean was calm, surfers would ask the *kahuna* (priest) help them pray for the gods to deliver bigger waves to them.

The kahuna would also help the surfers build a surfboard. The surfer would choose a tree, which they would dig out. They'd place a fish in the hole, which they offered to the gods. Craftsmen would shape, stain, and prepare the board. There were three shapes: the 'olo (thick in the middle and narrow towards the edges), the kiko'o (12 to18 feet long), and the alaia (9 feet long and required a lot of skill).

Kahalu'u Bay and Holualoa Bay were popular ancient surfing spots, which can still be accessed today.

After people from the Western world immigrated to Hawaii, they brought diseases with them. Colonization began to take place. Native Hawaiians were put to work on sugar plantations, and missionaries began to convert Hawaiians into Christians. Surfing and many other aspects of the native Hawaiian culture were lost in the process.

Surfing began to regain popularity after Waikiki became a tourist attraction. When wealthy Americans came to the beach, they saw locals surfing and wanted to experience it themselves. Famous authors took an interest. In 1886, Mark Twain tried to surf, but he failed. Jack London also tried it, even writing about it an essay that was published as "A Royal Sport" in 1907.

Alexander Hume Ford established the Outrigger Canoe and Surfing Club in 1908. The local Hawaiians founded their own club in 1911, which they called Hui Nalu ("Club of the Waves").

George Freeth and Duke Kahanamoku became the first major surf icons to be recognized throughout the world. Duke Kahanamoku Beach in Waikiki is named in Kahanamoku's honor.

As the popularity of the new sport started to increase, Waikiki locals started offering surfing lessons for tourists. This resulted in the Waikiki Beach Boys, who were a group of native Hawaiians who spent their days at the beach teaching tourists how to surf. This led to surf culture. People began to dedicate their lives to living on or near the beach and spending as much time as they could riding the waves. Although it began in Hawaii, it began to spread to other locations, such as California, Australia, and South Africa.

The rest is history. Surfing is a popular sport that people take part in at both the professional and recreational levels. And we can thank the native Hawaiians for it all!

Professional Surfing Competitions Take Place in Hawaii

Considering surfing was invented in Hawaii, it only seems fitting that it's home to some of the most important professional surfing competitions in the world.

The first international surfing contest in Hawaii was held in Makaha, located on western Oahu. The contest, known as the Makaha International Surfing

Championship, took place in 1954. The event was held every November or December until 1971. It was considered the "unofficial world championships."

Today, the top professional surfing competition in the world takes place in North Shore on Oahu. The competition is considered the "mecca of professional surfing."

It started out in 1971 when former world champion surfer Fred Hemmings staged the first Pipe Masters Event (which was first known as the "Hawaiian Masters"). There were six surfers, 10 folding chairs, and $1,000 in prize money. This small competition helped Hemmings recognize the potential of hosting surfing competitions in North Shore, so in 1983, he went on to organize the Triple Crown of Surfing.

Hemmings created a professional surfing title in Hawaii and three surfing events: The Pipe Masters, the World Cup of Surfing, and the Hawaiian Pro. In the beginning, only male surfers were able to compete. There's now a female competition offered as well. The competition is what we now know as the Vans Triple Crown of Surfing.

Many Professional Surfers Hail from Hawaii

It may come as no surprise to learn that many professional surfers were born and raised in Hawaii. Some of the most famous surfers from the state include:

- Duke "The Duke" Kahanamoku: Considered as the "forefather of professional surfing," there's a nine-foot bronze statue in honor of the late Kahanamoku at Waikiki beach.
- Andy Irons: The Kauai native won three world titles and more than 20 international victories before passing away in 2010.
- Keala Kennelly: Kennelly, who is considered to be one of the best female surfers of all time, is from Kauai.
- Coco Ho: Born in Honolulu, Coco Ho comes from a family of professional surfers. Her father Michael Ho and her uncle Derek Ho both had successful professional surfing careers.
- Carol Phillips: Hawaiian-born Phillips was the first female surfer to compete against men at Hawaii's Banzai Pipeline. She also founded the North Shore Surf Girls – Surf School.
- Brian Keaulana: Born and raised in Oahu, the professional surfer has worked as a stunt coordinator for many movies, including *50 First Dates, Jurassic World*, and *Memoirs of a Geisha*.

These are just some of the most well-known surfers from the Aloha State!

One of the Most Inspiring People of All-Time is From the Aloha State

Professional surfer Bethany Hamilton is, by far, one of the most inspirational people of all-time.

Bethany Hamilton, who was born and raised in Kauai, began surfing when she was just eight years old. In 2013, thirteen-year-old Hamilton was attacked by a tiger shark while she was surfing with her best friend. Hamilton survived the attack, but she tragically lost her left arm in the attack.

Hamilton didn't let a shark attack stop her from surfing, though. She returned to the sport about a month after losing her arm.

In 2014, Bethany Hamilton won first place in the Pipeline Women's Pro.

Today, Hamilton is a mother and a role model for both surfers and people throughout the world. She wrote a book about her journey, titled *Soul Surfer: A True Story of Faith, Family, and Fighting to Get Back on the Board*.

Hamilton's book was adapted into a film called *Soul Surfer*, which featured actress AnnaSophia Robb as Bethany. The 2011 movie also starred Helen Hunt, Dennis Quaid, and Carrie Underwood. While the film received mixed reviews, it brought attention to Hamilton's struggles and inspirational journey.

A Cult Classic Surfing Movie Was Filmed in Hawaii

The cult classic surfing film, *Blue Crush*, was filmed in Hawaii. The movie features Kate Bosworth, Michelle Rodriguez, and Sanoe Lake, who star as friends who are aspiring to be surfers on Oahu's North Shore. The movie was mostly filmed on location, with some scenes also being filmed at the Hawaii Film Studio in Honolulu.

A number of professional surfers made appearances in *Blue Crush*. Some of these include Keala Kennelly, Carol Phillips, Coco Ho, Rochelle Ballard, Layne Beachley, Megan Abubo, Brian Keaulana.

Blue Crush 2 was a sequel that went straight to video. While it's technically considered a sequel, the movie is completely unrelated to the original *Blue Crush*. The movie received negative reviews.

As of 2017, *NBC* announced that it was working on developing a TV series based on the original film.

There Are No Professional Sports Teams in Hawaii

It may (or may not) surprise you to learn that there are no professional sports teams in Hawaii. This is mostly due to logistical reasons. It would be too complicated (and expensive) to transport players to and from the state for games.

Hawaii *does* have college sports teams, however. The state has been home to college football bowl games over the years. The Poi Bowl, which was later renamed the Pineapple Bowl, used to take place at Honolulu Stadium. The games were then moved to Aloha Stadium in Honolulu and the name of the bowl was changed to the Aloha Bowl. Since 2002, the game, which continues to take place at Aloha Stadium, is called the Hawaii Bowl.

An NFL Player is From Hawaii

Did you know that one NFL player hails from Hawaii?

Manti Te'o is from Laei on the island of Oahu. He attended Punahou School in the Manoa neighborhood of Honolulu where he played football. Te'o was named the Gatorade state player of the year in 2007 when he was a junior.

By his senior year, Te'o was considered to be one of the best recruits at both the state and national level. In 2008, he led the Punahou football team to its first state championship.

To this day, Manti Te'o is considered Hawaii's most highly recruited athlete of all-time.

Te'o was recruited by the Notre Dame Fighting Irish, though he also had offers from Brigham Young and Southern California.

Teo played for the Fighting Irish from 2009 to 2012.

In 2013, Teo was drafted by the San Diego Chargers. In 2017, he was drafted by the New Orleans Saints.

And it all started out in Laei on Oahu!

RANDOM FACTS

1. The TV series *Lost* was filmed mostly on location on the island of Oahu. Between its location and large cast, the show was one the most expensive TV series of all-time to produce. The pilot episode alone cost $14 million.

2. The late musician Don Ho was born in Honolulu. The Hawaiian musician was most well-known for his song "Tiny Bubbles." He also guest-starred in TV series, such as *The Brady Bunch*, *I Dream of Jeannie*, *Charlie's Angels*, *Batman*, and more.

3. Don Ho's daughter, Hoku, was also a musician at one point. Widely regarded as a two-hit wonder, she was most well-known for her song "Another Dumb Blonde," as well as "Perfect Day," which was featured on the *Legally Blonde* movie soundtrack.

4. Actress Janell Parrish lived in Honolulu until she was 14 years old. Her family moved her to Los Angeles so that she could pursue her acting career. She rose to fame with her role as Mona Vanderwaal in the TV series *Pretty Little Liars*.

5. One of the actresses from *Gilmore Girls* was born in Hawaii! Lauren Graham, who is best known

for her role as Lorelei Gilmore, is from Honolulu. Graham moved to Virginia with her father when her parents divorced when she was five years old.

6. Actor Tahj Mowry was born in Honolulu, Hawaii! His famous older sisters, Tia and Tamera (of *Sister Sister* fame), were not born in the state.

7. Bill Gates and Melinda French got married on the island of Lanai back in 1994! The couple said their "I Do's" at the Four Seasons Resort Lanai. The resort's par-72 links, which are built on lava outcroppings, offer scenic views of the Pacific Ocean. Bill Gate and Melinda French said their vows at the par-3 12th hole, where you can hold an intimate ceremony of up to 13 people.

8. Musician Jack Johnson is from the North Shore in Oahu. He began surfing at five years old and competed in the Pipeline Masters. Johnson's surfing career didn't last for long, however. He had a surfing accident at the Pipeline, which caused him to lose teeth and need over 150 forehead stitches. His surfing accident was the inspiration of his song "Drink the Water."

9. Author Lois Lowry was born in Honolulu, Hawaii. The author is most well-known for her book *The Giver*, which was adapted into a dystopian film of the same name in 2014.

10. The *CBS* TV series *Hawaii Five-0* is set in Hawaii. Many scenes are filmed in Oahu, which may come as no surprise, considering the *Hawaii Five-0* team is supposed to be stationed in Honolulu.

11. Actor Tom Selleck lived in Hawaii while he was filming the show *Magnum, P.I.*

12. Actress Kristina Anapau was born in Hawaii. Anapau is most well-known for her role as Maurella in the show *True Blood*. She also played in the movie *Black Swan.*

13. NFL player Marcus Mariota was born in Honolulu. Mariota played high school football at the Saint Louis School in Honolulu. He later went on to play college football for the Oregon Ducks. Mariota won the Heisman Trophy in 2014. He was drafted by the Tennessee Titans of the NFL in 2015.

14. Carrie Ann Inaba, who's most known for being a judge on the show *Dancing with the Stars*, was born and raised in Honolulu. Inaba attended the Punahou School.

15. Actress Roseanne Barre, who starred in the hit sitcom *Roseanne*, owns a macadamia farm on the Big Island. She had a short-lived reality show called *Roseanne's Nuts*, which aired on *Lifetime*, about her farm.

16. Actor Beau Bridges attended the University of Hawaii.

17. Kelly Preston is from Honolulu. The actress's middle name is "Kamalelehua," which means "garden of lehuas." A lehua is a Hawaiian flower. Preston attended the Punahou School. She's most well-known for her marriage to John Travolta.

18. Nicole Scherzinger, who was the lead singer for the former girl band the Pussycat Dolls, was born in Honolulu.

19. Former Beatles member George Harrison once lived in Hawaii.

20. The Disney animated film *Moana* is believed to be based on Hawaii, though it's not specifically stated where the film takes place. Most of the cast members of the film, including Nicole Scherzinger and Dwayne Johnson, have ties to Hawaii.

Test Yourself – Questions and Answers

1. Which actress bought a plane ticket with her earnings for a role as an extra for a movie she played in while living in Hawaii?

   a. Nicole Kidman
   b. Nicole Scherzinger
   c. Bette Midler

2. Which Disney movie is thought to take place in Hawaii?

   a. *Moana*
   b. *The Little Mermaid*
   c. *The Princes and the Frog*

3. Which famous musician was raised by a musical family in Honolulu?

   a. Adam Levine
   b. Bruno Mars
   c. Michael Jackson

4. Which inspirational person is from Hawaii?

   a. Kim Kardashian
   b. Oprah Winfrey
   c. Bethany Hamilton

5. Which *Gilmore Girls* actress was born in Hawaii?

   a. Alexis Bledel
   b. Lauren Graham
   c. Kelly Bishop

Answers

1. c.
2. a.
3. b.
4. c.
5. b.

CHAPTER FOUR

HAWAII'S INVENTIONS, IDEAS, AND MORE!

Have you ever wondered what inventions you can thank Hawaii for? Do you know what products are most commonly produced in the Aloha State? Hawaii is known for a number of products, ideas, and other inventions. Do you know which form of dance originated from Hawaii and how it's different in modern times? Do you know which piece of athletic equipment originated from the state? Do you know which food-related invention helped shape the pineapple industry into what it is today? Do you know which famous cocktail originated from the state and why? To find out what we can credit the state of Hawaii for, read on!

Hula

When you think of planning a vacation to Hawaii, it's hard not to think of a hula girl. It may already be a given that hula started out in Hawaii. The style of dance plays a key role in native Hawaiian culture. But do you know how different hula in modern times is from the traditional style of hula dance? Do you know what hula is really about?

There are a lot of misconceptions about traditional hula dance. What many of us think of as hula dance is the Westernized version. Hula dancers traditionally didn't wear a grass skirt, lei, and coconut shell bra. In fact, the coconut shell bra wasn't ever worn by natives. This was a commercialized invention to attract tourists and add to the overall "sex appeal" of the Hawaiian girl. Although natives did wear grass skirts, it wasn't always that way. In the 1800s, the native Hawaiians were inspired by the natives of Kiribati (then the Gilbert Islands), who first introduced grass skirts to the region. The Hawaiian natives decided to make their own version of the grass skirt.

Hula is about more than outfits. Traditionally, it's a way for native Hawaiians to pass stories and history down to younger generations.

Hula is considered to be a religious dance, as natives traditionally danced in honor or celebration of a Hawaiian god or goddess. Traditionally, it was considered to be a token of bad luck or might even have negative consequences to make a mistake. When hula dancers were learning the dance, they were excluded from performing in rituals and were believed to be under the protection of Laka, the goddess of hula.

An old Hawaiian legend has it that hula originated on the island of Molokai. It's been said that Laka gave birth to the dance at a sacred place in Ka'ana on Molokai.

In reality, hula was developed by the Polynesians who settled on the islands. While there are dances similar to other Polynesian islands, the hula dance is unique to Hawaii itself.

Today, Ka Hula Piko takes place on Molokai island. It's an event that honors hula's origins with dancing, storytelling, food, and more. Ka Hula Piko takes place every year.

Kona Coffee

Did you know that Hawaii is the *only* state in the United States that grows coffee, cocoa, and vanilla beans at the commercial level? The weather conditions in the state, along with the minerals found in volcanic soil, have made Hawaii ideal for coffee-growing conditions.

Kona Coffee is the name that's used to describe coffee that's grown in the Kona District of Hawaii. All of the coffee from the district is handpicked, wet-method pressed, and sun-dried. Between that and the climate conditions, it's said to have a unique taste.

Kona Coffee is said to be some of the most expensive coffee in the entire world!

With more than 600 farms in the Kona District that produce coffee, you might be surprised to learn that no two Kona Coffee blends taste the same.

Some of the most popular brands of Kona Coffee include Hula Daddy Kona Coffee, Volcanica Coffee, Moki's Farm, Hawaiian Queen Coffee, and Kona Gold Rum Co.

The Modern Surfboard

Considering surfing got its start in Hawaii, it may come as no surprise to learn that the modern, lightweight surfboard also originated from the state.

Surfer Tom Blake is responsible for what we now know as the modern-day surfboard. Blake spent some time perfecting his design. It took him multiple attempts to get it right. He was first credited with designing the hollow surfboard. He drilled hundreds of holes into the wooden boards. Prior to Blake's hollow surfboards, boards had weighed up to 200 pounds. His design opened up new possibilities for people who were unable to carry such heavy boards.

However, wooden boards were eventually suspended. They were replaced by laminated boards and then, eventually, foam and fiberglass boards. These boards still weren't perfect, leading Blake to continue to see a need for a lighter board.

In 1935, Blake was the first to add a fin to the surfboard, which had traditionally been flat-bottomed before that. He did this by fastening the keel from an old speedboat to a surfboard.

The Pineapple Coring Machine

Have you ever wondered who to thank for those pre-cored pineapples you find at the grocery store? What about those cups of pineapple fruit?

Well, the credit goes to Henry Ginaca, who invented the pineapple coring machine back in 1911.

Hawaiian pineapple magnate James Dole asked Henry Ginaca, an engineer, to design a machine that would automatically peel and core pineapples.

His invention came to be known as the Ginaca machine. The machine completely changed the fruit canning industry and increased overall pineapple production.

Ocean Vodka

Ocean Vodka is a spirit that's handcrafted in Hawaii. This vodka is unique for several reasons. It's the only spirit in the entire world that's made from deep ocean mineral water. The high content of the minerals gives the vodka a unique flavor. It's also the only vodka that's distilled from organic sugar cane.

Hawaiian Airlines has been exclusively serving Ocean Vodka since 2007.

The Ocean Vodka Organic Farm & Distillery is located on the island of Maui.

The No Billboards Policy

Okay, so this isn't so much of an invention as it is an idea, but Hawaii was the first one to come up with it.

In 1927, Hawaii became the first state to ever ban billboards. This was done to preserve the state's natural beauty.

Although Hawaii was the first start to think of it, they're not the only state who's banned billboards. Four other states—all of which are recognized for their natural beauty—have followed suit. In addition to Hawaii, you also won't find billboards in Alaska, Maine, and Vermont, either.

"Cropsticks"

You've probably heard of chopsticks, but have you ever heard of "Cropsticks"?

Mylen Fe Yamamoto, who graduated from Moanalua High School, is the inventor of Cropsticks. The idea is pretty simple. Cropsticks act like regular chopsticks, but they have a detachable platform on each side that is designed to keep them from rolling off the table. Yamamoto has said she got the idea for her invention when her chopsticks rolled off her tray table on a plane while she was traveling to Asia.

As an added bonus, Cropsticks are eco-friendly. They're made from sustainable bamboo.

Yamamoto took her invention to the show *Shark Tank*, but she failed to get any of the Sharks to invest in her product.

The Ukulele

The Ukulele plays an integral role in Hawaiian music and culture. The instrument's rise to popularity in the Hawaiian culture had a lot to do with King Kalakaua, who was a big fan of the instrument. He incorporated the ukulele into performances at royal gatherings.

The instrument was designed by a man named Manuel Nunes. Originally from Portugal, Nunes and his friends immigrated to Honolulu to work on the sugar cane fields. Manuel Nunes designed the ukulele, which he based on several Portuguese guitar-like instruments. He had the help of two of his friends: José do Espírito Santo and Augusto Dias. Just two weeks after the men arrived in Hawaii in 1879, the *Hawaiian Gazette* reported that they were entertaining people with nightly street concerts.

The word *ukulele* translates to "jumping flea." It's believed that the instrument was given this name because of the way you must move your fingers around a lot to play it. It's believed that one of King Kalakaua's officers, Edward William Purvis, may have been the inspiration of the name. Purvis, who played the instrument, was allegedly small and fidgety.

Hawaiian Shirts

Have you ever wondered if Hawaiian shirts, which are also known as Aloha shirts, originated from Hawaii? The name almost seems so obvious that you would think they actually started out in Oklahoma or some unexpected state. Well, sorry to disappoint you, but Hawaiian shirts did originate from the Aloha State.

The Hawaiian shirts you probably know of today are not what's sold to Hawaii natives and locals. Traditional men's Aloha shirts have prints that contain Hawaiian quilt patterns and typically come in muted colors. Hawaiian shirts that are marketed at tourists tend to come in brighter shades and have prints that may consist of floral, palm tree, surfboard, or other tropical elements.

Aloha shirts date back to the early 1900s when the first shirt was sold by a shop run by Japanese immigrants in Honolulu. The first Aloha shirt was handsewn from Japanese kimono fabrics.

A Chinese immigrant named Ellery Chun later went on to develop what we currently know as the modern Hawaiian shirt. Chun sold the shirts from his store, which was called King-Smith Clothiers and Dry Goods in Waikiki. Chun's shirts were first sold in 1935.

After World War II, many servicemen went back to the United States wearing Hawaiian shirts. This sparked interest in the style. Tourists began to go to Hawaii in the 1950s and purchased the shirts.

Alfred Shaheen, a textile manufacturer, began to mass produce Hawaiian shirts. Elvis Presley wore a red Hawaiian shirt produced by Alfred Shaheen on the cover of the *Blue Hawaii* movie soundtrack in 1961, which really helped popularize the style.

Today, you can find Hawaiian shirts at various retailers throughout the United States, including Wal-Mart. But there's nothing quite like a Hawaiian shirt from the Aloha State!

Tiki Statues

When you think of Hawaii, you probably think of Tiki statues. What you might not know is that Tiki statues play a key role in native Hawaiian culture. The Polynesians brought this aspect of their culture to Hawaii when they migrated to the islands.

The cultural beliefs surrounding tiki statues is very interesting. According to Maori (native New Zealand) mythology, Tiki is the name of the first man in existence. The stone or wooden statues, which are called tiki statues, are meant to represent either Tiki himself or the spirits of other people.

The native Hawaiians had their own beliefs on who "Tiki" really was. In fact, they didn't believe the first man went by the name Tiki at all. What they believed was that Kumuhonua was the first man to ever exist. They believed he was made by Kāne, or by Kāne, Kū, and Lono, the Hawaiian gods. The Hawaiians believed that Kumuhonua's body was made by mixing red earth with saliva. They believed that Kāne carried earth from the four corners of the world, which led Kumuhonua to be shaped like Kāne himself.

When you visit Hawaii, you'll be bound to see tiki statues throughout the state. Although they're now there in part because tourists expect them, their meaning really runs so much deeper within the native Hawaii culture!

Blue Hawaii Cocktail

If you're ever at a tiki bar, you'll probably see the Blue Hawaii cocktail on the menu. You might be wondering who you can thank for this fruity alcoholic beverage.

The Blue Hawaii was created at the Hilton Hawaiian Village (which was then known as the Hawaiian Village Hotel) in Waikiki in the late 1950s. It was invented by Harry Yee, who was the head bartender at the hotel for over 30 years.

Harry Yee was approached by a sales representative who asked him to design a drink that contained blue Curacao liqueur. The idea was to create a drink that would get the liqueur popular enough to sell.

Yee experimented with several different concoctions when designing the drink, and there are a few variations out there today. The most popular version of the Blue Hawaiian contains rum, pineapple juice, Blue Curacao, sweet and sour mix, a pineapple wedge, and a cocktail umbrella. In some versions of the recipe, vodka is also added.

You might think the drink was named after Elvis Presley's movie *Blue Hawaii*, but you'd be mistaken. Yee named the drink the "Blue Hawaii" after the song "Blue Hawaii" by Leo Robin for the movie *Waikiki Wedding*, which starred Bing Crosby.

While the Blue Hawaiian might be Harry Yee's most well-known accomplishment, it wasn't his only invention. In addition to creating Hawaii's most legendary cocktail, Yee also created the Banana Daquiri and the Tropical Itch.

The Banana Daiquiri is made the same as a traditional daiquiri (rum, lime juice, and sugar), mixed with half of a banana.

The Tropical Itch is made from 151 rum, bourbon, passion fruit juice, and triple sec. Dark rum is added on top of the drink, along with bitters. Afterwards, the drink is garnished with a tall bamboo backscratcher.

In addition to concocting these famous cocktails, Harry Yee also played a vital role in shaping the faux tiki and tiki bar culture in Hawaiian. Yee's rum drinks and hula girls added to the Hawaiian tiki bar culture we know of today.

Shave Ice

Today, it's a popular summertime sweet treat, but did you know that shave ice originated from the Aloha State? While shave ice didn't start out in Hawaii, its origins in the United States did.

Shave ice was imported to Hawaii by Japanese immigrants, who brought it with them when they came to the region to work in sugar plantations. Shave ice (and snow cones) both quickly became a part of Hawaiian culture.

Similar to a snow cone, shave ice (or Hawaiian shave ice) is made by shaving an ice block. On the Big Island of Hawaii, it's sometimes called "ice shave." Flavored syrups are added to the shave ice, which is traditionally served in a cone-shaped paper or plastic cup. The only real difference between shave ice and a snow cone is that crushed ice is used when preparing snow cones.

Throughout most of the country, traditional American flavored syrups in flavors like grape and cherry are usually added to shave ice. In Hawaii, however, you can expect to find different flavoring options. Local ingredients are generally used to flavor shave ice. Some of these ingredients generally include guava, lychee, kiwi fruit, mango, pineapple, passion fruit, and coconut cream. Multiple flavors are generally added, as well as vanilla ice cream and/or adzuki bean paste. A "snow cap" (or sweetened condensed milk) may be drizzled on top. Shave ice is really popular on the North Shore of Oahu, Maui, and the Big Island.

Hawaiian Pizza

Have you ever wondered where the world's most controversial pizza came from? Well, it might surprise you to learn that Hawaiian pizza was *not* invented in Hawaii. Despite the pizza's name, Sam Panopoulos was originally from Greece and lived in Ontario, Canada when he came up with the idea of putting pineapple on a pizza with ham or bacon at his family's restaurant.

That being said, Hawaii *did* indirectly have some role in the invention—and that's in its name. Panopoulos said the pie was named after the brand of canned pineapple he and his brothers used at their restaurant. The Hawaiian Pineapple Company is located in Kunia on the island of Oahu. It's strange to think that Hawaiian Pizza could have been Dole Pizza if Panopoulos had used a different brand of pineapple.

Pineapple Jack-O-Lanterns

Have you ever wondered what people in Hawaii decorate their front porches with on Halloween?

While people from the contiguous United States carve pumpkins this Halloween, many Hawaiians will be carving pineapple Jack-O-Lanterns. With pineapples being so plentiful throughout the state, it's easier for Hawaiians to get their hands on one than pumpkins—though, it's worth noting that there *are* pumpkin patches in the Aloha State.

But pineapple Jack-O-Lanterns are more commonly found throughout Hawaii, and they're pretty cool looking!

Halloween in the Aloha State is known as the "Mardi Gras of the Pacific," by the way!

Sea Salt

Although sea salt is derived from a number of places, it is harvested from the oceans that surround Hawaii.

Red sea salt is specific to Hawaii. It gets its color from red clay that gets baked into the sea salt due to

Hawaii's volcanoes. Traditionally, native Hawaiians used red sea salt, which they called *'alaea*, in purification ceremonies.

Black sea salt also comes from the oceans surrounding Hawaii. The color comes from powdered black lava.

RANDOM FACTS

1. A company called CBI Polymers, which is based in Honolulu, designed a gel technology that can be used to mop radioactive particles.

2. The hooked cane knife was invented by a Norwegian who immigrated to Hawaii.

3. A Hawaii local named Norman Texeira designed the first machine that was able to clean beaches. The machine was able to clean the beach overnight.

4. Tom Blake, the inventor of the surfboard, is also credited with designing the sailboard while living in Hawaii. Blake did this by attaching a sail to one of his surfboards. In his earliest design, he used an umbrella.

5. Blake also invented the paddleboard for rescue use. Known as the "aluminum 'torpedo' rescue buoy," his design has been said to save thousands of lives.

6. Tom Blake was also responsible for inventing a waterproof camera housing, which allowed him to take underwater photographs. Although there had been multiple attempts to design an underwater camera, Blake's design was significant. It was even recognized by *National Geographic* in 1935.

7. The "SpeedSafe" assisted opening mechanism for Kershaw Knives was invented by a Kaneohe local. The inventor, Kenneth J. Onion, was an award-winning knifemaker.

8. Joseph Kekuku, who was from Oahu, invented the Hawaiian steel guitar. He accidentally stumbled upon the invention while he was attending Kamehameha School for Boys in Honolulu.

9. Spam musubi is a recipe that originated from Hawaii. It's basically sushi, but the Spam is used in place of raw fish. Spam is a staple food among Hawaiian locals, with the most Spam consumed per capita in the United States. Therefore, there are a number of ways people throughout the state eat the food. Spam is eaten on burgers, pizza, in fried rice, with ramen, and a number of other ways.

10. The Maui Gold Brand of pineapple is recognized for its uniqueness and superiority to other pineapples. It takes 18 months to reach full ripeness, but it contains triple the amount of Vitamin C as other brands do.

11. POG juice comes from Hawaii. "POG" stands for "passion, orange, guava." The juice is served on Hawaiian Airlines and can be found throughout the Aloha State.

12. The hashtag #LuckyWeLiveHI was created by the people of Hawaii. Many people who live in the state consider the hashtag to be their motto.

13. Macadamia nuts are one of Hawaii's biggest crops. You'll find all types of macadamia nuts throughout the Big Island, ranging from chocolate covered macadamia nuts to macadamia nut butter. Macadamia nut oil is also very popular in the state.

14. Black pearls, which come from the Pacific Ocean, can be frequently found throughout Hawaiian jewelry stores. Coral jewelry is also popular in Hawaii.

15. The Shaka is a hand symbol that's used throughout the Hawaiian Islands. It's popular among surfers. To make this hand sign, the pointer finger, middle finger, and ring finger should be folded down towards your palm. The thumb and pinkie finger will stay up. You'll rotate your hand so that your palm is facing you. The most common meaning of this hand symbol is "what's up, bro?"

16. Tea is grown in Hawaii. In fact, Hawaii is the largest U.S. state for tea production. Mauna Kea Tea and the Onomea Tea Company both produce tea blends in the state.

17. Researchers in Norway have found that people on a tiny Polynesian island called Mangareva,

which is roughly 5,000 kilometers south of Hawaii, were the first to do binary math. When these people immigrated to Hawaii, it's likely that they brought their binary number system with them.

18. Puka shell necklaces were originally made from the bead-like shells of sea snails in Hawaii. The necklaces eventually came to be manufactured by companies that designed them to look like the shells. Puka shell necklaces were popular in the 1990s.

19. Muumuu dresses originated in Hawaii. Similar to Hawaiian shirts, they're generally worn in more muted colors among Hawaiian locals and tend to be favored in bright colors by tourists. The word *mu'umu'u* means "cut off" in Hawaiian, which is because the original style of the dress didn't have a yoke. It was originally designed as a shorter, less formal version of the holoku dress, which was worn by Protestant missionaries who came to Hawaii during the 1820s.

20. Hōkūle'as, or double-hulled voyaging canoes, originated in Polynesia and, within the United States, Hawaii.

Test Yourself – Questions and Answers

1. Under Native Hawaiian beliefs, Laka is the goddess of:

   a. Leis
   b. Tiki
   c. Hula

2. Tom Blake did _not_ invent which of the following?

   a. Modern surfboards
   b. Waterproof camera housing
   c. Boogey boards

3. Hawaiian shirts were originally made from:

   a. Muumuu dresses
   b. Kimono fabric
   c. Bird feathers

4. The hand symbol that's popular in Hawaii surf culture is known as the ____.

   a. Shaka
   b. Sharka
   c. Swanka

5. One of the most popular food items in Hawaii is:

   a. Spam
   b. Bacon
   c. Breakfast cereal

Answers

1. c.

2. c.

3. b.

4. a.

5. a.

CHAPTER FIVE

HAWAII'S ATTRACTIONS

If you're thinking about planning a visit to the Aloha State, you might be wondering what attractions the islands have to offer. But how much do you really know about what there is to see and do in Hawaii? Do you know what the No. 1 most popular tourist attraction in the Aloha State is? Do you know which famous (and hard to find) famous treat can be found in Hawaii and where? Do you know which attraction holds the record as being the second oldest operating facility of its kind in the entire country? To learn the answers to these questions and other fun facts about Hawaii's attractions, read on!

You Can Actually Feel Volcanic Activity at Hawaii Volcanoes National Park

Have you ever wanted to experience what volcanic activity feels like? If so, then Hawaii Volcanoes National Park, located on the Big Island, is an absolute must-see.

You can get a close-up, first-hand look at Kilauea, which has been active for years. You'll see lava seeping from the earth's fissures. You'll get to walk on the surrounding land, which has been molded by cooled lava rock.

The coolest part about Hawaii Volcanoes National Park is when there's a lot of volcanic activity in the area. Tourists actually have the opportunity of feeling this activity. You might feel seismic activity, hear the sound of gas emissions booming, or be able to witness ash being released into the air. It's an experience unlike any other.

But don't worry. Your safety is a top priority. If Kilauea is *too* active, you'll be restricted from seeing areas of the park.

Some of the other things you'll find in the park include Thurston Lava Tube (a lava cave), the Hawaiian Volcano Observatory, and the Devastation Trail.

Mauna Kea Isn't for Amateur Hikers

If you'll recall, the Big Island's volcano Mauna Kea's 13,802-foot peak makes it the highest point in all of Hawaii and the second-highest point above sea level of *any* island on Earth. If you're into hiking, chances are you might want to explore the dormant volcano's peak, but you might want to reconsider that.

It's recommended that only the most experienced of hikers should try to hike Mauna Kea. This is due to the changes in altitude. In fact, it's been estimated that about one out of 3 visitors tends to experience altitude sickness when climbing to the volcano's summit.

It's recommended that you stop for *at least* 30 minutes at the visitor center in order to allow your body to adjust to the changes in altitude. The visitor center can be found at about 9,200 feet and offers stargazing opportunities in the evening.

If you're thinking about driving to the highest summit of the volcano, it's recommended that you only use a four-wheel drive vehicle. Just keep in mind that there's no fuel available on Mauna Kea and brakes tend to overheat on the way down.

It's also worth noting that the volcano's summit is very cold during the months of winter when the summit is covered in snow.

Don't worry, though. This all may sound discouraging, but you *can* safely see the summit of Mauna Kea. Each year, an estimated 5,000 to 6,000 visitors make the trip. In order to make sure this is done safely, there are park rangers available for your assistance.

"The Grand Canyon of the Pacific" is in Hawaii

Did you know that Waimea Canyon is known as the "Grand Canyon of the Pacific"?

Located on the western side of Kauai, the canyon spans across 10 miles in length and has areas where it's as deep as 3,600 feet. At some points, Waimea Canyon is also a mile wide.

The word *Waimea* means "reddish water." This is referring to the red-toned soil of the canyon, which was caused by erosion.

You'll also find waterfalls at Waimea Canyon, as well as hiking trails and rafting tours at the nearby Kokee State Park.

You Can Have Encounters with Sea Turtles in Hawaii

In Hawaiian, turtles are known as *honu*. Did you know there are a couple of places throughout the state where you can have encounters with honu?

The Maui Ocean Center offers Turtle Lagoon, where you can have close encounters with green sea turtles. The green sea turtle, which is native to Hawaii, can be as long as four feet and weigh more than 300 pounds. You can see up to six green sea turtles on display at Turtle Lagoon. The Maui Ocean Center is also home to a number of other types of marine life, including sharks, stingrays, thousands of fish, and more.

If you want to see some sea turtles in their natural habitat, then you might consider visiting Ali'i Beach Park, which is located on Oahu's North Shore. There are known to be a lot of sea turtles throughout the park.

Turtle Beach, which is also located on the North Shore, is another popular place to find sea turtles. The turtles are known to come close to the shore, but they don't always come out to visit.

If you're trying to see some sea turtles in the wild, remember to look and not *touch!* Touching and handling the sea turtles is illegal, so you'll just want to take pictures of them and appreciate them from afar.

The Dole Plantation is One of the Only Places in the World Where You Can Try This

Located in Wailua on Oahu, the Dole Plantation first opened as a fruit stand back in 1950. In 1989, the plantation opened to the public to offer visitors a "Pineapple Experience." Today, the Dole Plantation is one of the most popular tourist attractions on Oahu and sees more than one million visitors per year!

You can ride the Pineapple Express Train Tour, which is a 20-minute train ride that will teach you more about the history of Hawaii's most beloved fruit and how James Dole established his pineapple empire.

You can take the Plantation Garden Tour, where you'll get to explore the plantation's eight gardens. This is where Dole grows its cacao pods, coffee, and exotic fruits.

Perhaps one of the coolest parts about the Dole Plantation is its Pineapple Garden Maze. In 2008, the maze was named the largest maze in the world. The maze, which is shaped like a pineapple and made from 14,000 Hawaiian plants, spans across 2.5 miles (or three acres) of land.

A trip to the Dole Plantation isn't complete without a trip to the Plantation Grille. You'll find unique island and pineapple-inspired menu items (and traditional American fare, too). But what you'll want to try while you're there is Dole Whip! The Dole Plantation is one of the only places in the world (as well as Disney Parks) where you can find the soft-serve, dairy-free frozen dessert.

This Beach Town is Home to a Unique Walking Trail and a U.S. Monument

Waikiki Beach is one of the most popular beach towns for tourists to visit. A suburb of Honolulu, it's most well-known for its tourist resorts, restaurants, and the Waikiki Beach Walk, where you'll find cafes and entertainment venues.

But one of the most unique aspects of the beach town is the Waikiki Historic Trail. The trail has historic markers, which are made of surfboards. This is in honor of Waikiki's own (now deceased) Olympic gold medalist and famed surfer Duke Kahanamoku.

Another one of the town's must-sees is the Diamond Head State Monument, which is a volcanic tuff cone that's also a U.S. National Natural Monument. There, you'll find scenic views of the Pacific Ocean and Honolulu. The volcanic tuff cone once served as a post for the U.S. military that was used to prevent attacks on Honolulu.

There's also a trail that will lead you to the edge of the Diamond Head crater. The crater, which is estimated to be about 300,000 years old, is about 760-feet deep. The trail to get there isn't that long, but it's known to be a bit challenging due to its steepness. Hiking in the park is only allowed until 4:30 p.m. and the trail takes approximately 1.5 to 2 hours to hike.

Hawaii is Home to "The Wall of Tears"

Have you ever heard of the "Wall of Tears"?

Located on Mount Waialeale, the Wall of Tears was given its name because of the way hundreds of waterfalls "weep" from the mountain slopes. Found within the Napali Coast State Wilderness Park on the island of Kauai, there are a couple of ways you can witness this extraordinary sight. You can either approach it by water or you can take a helicopter tour for an aerial view.

There's also the Kalalau Trail. Encompassing eleven miles, the trail is only recommended to expert hikers.

Why Watching the Sun Rise at Haleakala is Popular Among Tourists

The Haleakala National Park sees more than 1.2 million visitors per year, making it one of Maui's top attractions. The park is home to Haleakala, the volcano which formed most of the island of Maui. Today, it's the largest dormant volcano in the world.

Within the 30,183 square acres that the park encompasses, you'll find a crater, a mountain, wilderness, and so much more. You'll find animals within the park, but keep in mind that the only animals that are actually native to the region are bats and seals. Everything else was brought to the park by men.

There are also 1,000 native species of flowers that can be found within the park. Of those, 90 percent can only be found within Hawaii.

Did you know that watching the sunrise at Haleakala is a popular activity among tourists? Do you know why?

The word *Haleakala* means "house of the sun." The volcano was given this name because the volcano's 10,023-foot peak, which is Maui's highest point, is known to be an incredible sight when the sun rises.

Sunrises at the Haleakala National Park are known to make for some truly beautiful photos.

You Can Cage Dive with Sharks on the North Shore

Have you ever dreamt of cage diving with a *manō*? (That's Hawaiian for shark). If so, you might want to check out North Shore Shark Adventures in Oahu.

The tour will take you from Haleiwa Small Boat Harbor. When you're two miles out to sea, you'll get to cage dive with sharks. The best part about it all is that shark encounters in Hawaii are completely *safe* — and thrilling!

The tour company will provide you with a mask and snorkel. Knowing how to swim isn't even necessary since you'll be holding onto bars while you float in the shark diving cage.

One of the added bonuses is that you'll also generally come across dolphins, Hawaiian green sea turtles, humpback whales, and other marine life during your journey.

Although there are other shark encounter tour companies, North Shore Shark Adventures was the first to begin operating in Hawaii. The company was founded in 2001.

Hawaii is Home to a Polynesian Cultural Center

With a state that's as rich in history as Hawaii, the Polynesian Cultural Center on Oahu is a must-see for any tourist. It's even been voted as Oahu's No. 1 attraction.

One of the most interesting aspects of the cultural center is the "villages" you will get to tour. Through these villages, you will be able to experience and learn more about the Islands of Aotearoa, the Island of Fiji, the Island of Samoa, the Island of Tahiti, and the Island of Tonga. Each village has something unique to teach you, such as how to fish without a net, how to toss a spear, and how to do traditional dances. You'll play ancient games, watch live cultural performances, and learn more about each island's culture.

The Polynesian Cultural Center also offers a traditional luau, which features a Polynesian buffet that includes menu items like Imu pork, teriyaki braised beef, poi, and chocolate haupia cake. You can enjoy your meal while watching a cultural song and dance.

After the luau, you'll get to enjoy a show called *Hā: Breath of Life*. The live nighttime performance features more than 100 Polynesian natives, who take part in song and dance to bring you a beautiful story.

The Honolulu Zoo Has a Unique History

Today, the Honolulu Zoo is one of the city's most popular family attractions, drawing in more than 600,000 visitors per year. But did you know that the zoo had a unique beginning?

In fact, the Honolulu Zoo is the only zoo in the United States that was originally established by sovereign Monarch grants. (Of course, this should come as no surprise, considering no other state in the U.S. was ever home to a monarchy).

The Honolulu Zoo opened back in 1877 and it wasn't a zoo at first. It was originally called the Queen Kapiolani Park and it was first opened to showcase King David Kalakaua's collection of birds. It also had a horse racing track when it first opened.

In 1914, Ben Hollinger, who served as the park director, took responsibility for the zoo. He began to add new animals to it, which included a monkey, a bear, and an African elephant.

Today, the zoo is still located within the Queen Kapiolani Park. It now encompasses 42 acres of land and is home to more than 1,200 animals. You'll find everything from lions and tigers to zebras and giraffes at the Honolulu Zoo.

You Can Take a Movie Tour at Kualoa Ranch

A number of movies have been filmed throughout the Ka'a'awa Valley. Did you know that you can take a movie tour to see where some of your favorite Hollywood movies have been filmed?

The Hollywood "Hawaii Backlot" tour, which is offered by Kualoa Ranch, gives you the opportunity to climb aboard a vintage school bus and see where some of your favorite movies and shows have been recorded. Some of the most famous include *Jurassic Park*, *Hawaii Five-0*, and *Lost*. In addition to seeing where some of your favorite movies and shows have been filmed, you'll also have the opportunity to see artifacts and memorabilia. You might even get to witness some filming as it takes place!

Kualoa Ranch has more to offer than the Hawaii Backlot tour. You can also take a Jungle Jeep Expedition tour or a horseback riding tour.

Kualoa Ranch also offers ATV tours. The ranch and its ATVs were featured in the movie *Mike and Dave Need Wedding Dates*, starring Zac Efron and Anna Kendrick.

Hawaii is Said to Have the Best Rainbows "On the Planet"

According to the *Huffington Post*, Hawaii might have the best rainbows on the planet. Rainbows are seen so frequently in the state that some people have even unofficially nicknamed Hawaii the "Rainbow State." Honolulu is known as the "Rainbow Capital of the World."

In the Hawaiian language, rainbows are called *aneune*, a word that originates from the goddess Aneune. She was said to be the messenger between the gods and the humans. Lore says that the goddess used rainbows as a road between the Earth and the heavens. The ancient Hawaiians also believed that rainbows were used as roads to heaven by people who had recently passed away.

Perhaps the best place to see rainbows in the state is at Wailuku River State Park: Located on the Big Island of Hawaii, the park's Rainbow Falls waterfall is one of the most popular places to go to see rainbows in the state. Rainbows are best seen there on sunny mornings.

That being said, regardless of where you go, you're bound to see rainbows. And you'll often see more than one! The best views of rainbows are often from higher points.

Aloha Tower is the "Statue of Liberty of Hawaii"

Aloha Tower, which is located at Pier 9 of Honolulu Harbor, is a lighthouse and one of Hawaii's landmarks.

The lighthouse has 10 stories and stands 184-feet tall with a 40-foot flag mast (for a total of 224 feet, total). For 40 years, the Aloha Tower was the tallest building in all of Hawaii. The tower's clock was one of the largest in all of the United States.

With its location near Waikiki, the Aloha Tower is still used as a docking port for cruise ships on the island. The most noteworthy ship that docks here is The Star of Honolulu. The lighthouse is also owned by Hawaii Pacific University and provides campus housing, restaurants, and more. There used to be shops nearby, but many of them have closed in recent years.

While the area is a great place to take in a lunch with a scenic view or experience live entertainment at night, the lighthouse has a history that might surprise you.

The Aloha Tower was built on September 11th, 1926. It cost a (then staggering) $160,000 to build. The tower was designed in the Hawaiian Gothic architectural style.

The tower's name is truly fitting: in the true "spirit of Aloha", the tower once greeted hundreds of thousands of immigrants to Honolulu the same way the Statue of Liberty once greeted hundreds of thousands to New York City.

Pearl Harbor is the No. 1 Tourist Attraction in Hawaii

If you're a history buff, then a trip to Hawaii isn't complete without a trip to Pearl Harbor. There are a number of things to see in honor of the tragedy.

The WWII Valor in the Pacific National Monument sees more than 1.8 million visitors from all over the world every year, making it the No. 1 most visited tourist attraction in Hawaii. At the Pearl Harbor monument, you'll find the USS *Arizona* Memorial, which was built over the sunken battleship, the USS *Arizona*. More than 1,170 people died aboard this ship during the attack on Pearl Harbor on December 7th, 1941. This accounts for more than half of the Americans who lost their lives during the tragedy.

Some of the other things to see at Pearl Harbor include the Battleship *Missouri* Memorial, the USS *Bowfin* Submarine Museum & Park, the Pacific Aviation Museum Pearl Harbor, and the Pearl Harbor Visitor Center.

You might be surprised to learn that people from Japan come to visit the Pearl Harbor memorial today. In fact, Japan is the largest source of international tourists who visit the attraction today. Japanese tourists visit the memorial to pay their respects, the same way people from the United States do. Japanese tourism plays a vital role in Hawaii's economics today.

RANDOM FACTS

1. You can learn more about coffee farming during your trip to Hawaii at the Kona Coffee Living History Farm. The farm is dedicated to preserving the history and traditions of coffee farming. You can explore the plantation, where coffee is still being produced today. You might also be able to see a Kona Nightingale. Other modern Kona coffee producers, such as Hula Daddy and Mountain Thunder Plantation, also offer plantation tours.

2. The Princeville Botanical Gardens, which is located in Princeville on Kauai, is a family-run facility. A tropical garden awaits you. You'll find everything from exotic flowers to medicinal plants here. The facility offers its popular Walking & Chocolate Tasting Tour. You'll have the chance to taste both raw cacao and gourmet chocolates, as well as honey (which is made from the nectar of the tropical flowers in the gardens) and seasonal fruit.

3. Hanauma Bay, which was formed in a volcanic crater on the island of Oahu, is a popular place to go snorkeling. At one point, the delicate reef ecosystem had begun to suffer, but it has since

been restored. The Hanauma Education Center provides education about the bay. There are also places to take snorkeling lessons so tourists can enjoy the bay's beautiful reefs.

4. Kamokila Village was once home to King Kaumualii, the last King of Kauai. Today, the traditional Hawaiian village has been recreated here. It's open to visitors to help them get a better understanding of how a traditional Hawaiian village worked hundreds of years ago. You'll learn more about the lifestyles of native Hawaiians, as well as have the chance to take part in canoe adventures.

5. Honolulu's Chinatown is one of its most famous attractions. With its location in downtown Honolulu, the 15-block district has a number of Southeastern Asian offerings. Some of the things you'll find include fresh produce, art galleries, bookstores, a bakery, retailers, and a café. There's also the Hawaiian Chinese Multicultural Museum & Archives, which is home to photographs and artifacts related to the area.

6. Manoa Falls is considered to be one of the most beautiful natural wonders of Honolulu, Oahu. You'll also be visiting "Jurassic Falls" from the *Jurassic Park* movie franchise when you decide to visit here. The waterfall, which is located in the Manoa Valley, has a 100-feet drop into a pool

below it. You can hike to the waterfall on the Manoa Falls Trail within about 30 minutes. Visitors are discouraged from swimming in the pool the waterfall falls into due to the risk of developing a Leptospirosis infection.

7. Waimea Bay Beach Park is every surfer's dream! The beach offers 20-foot waves, which aren't recommended for amateur surfers but are tame enough for most experienced surfers. Waimea Bay Beach Park has been ranked as one of the best big wave spots in the entire world more than once. The best time for surfers to ride the waves is during the winter months.

8. Hapuna Beach Park on the Big Island of Hawaii has been voted best beach in the U.S. more than once. In Hawaiian, *hapuna* means "pool" or "spring." It's one of the only white sand beaches on the Big Island. It's a popular place for snorkeling, thanks to a reef located at the southern point of the beach.

9. Molokini is a volcanic crater that's partially submerged. It forms a small islet, which has no residents, between the islands of Maui and Kahoolawe. Its crescent shape is ideal for scuba divers and snorkelers, as it protects them from the powerful waves and currents in the channel. There's a lush reef that can be seen 150-feet deep, where you will find more than 250 types of fish,

many of which are indigenous to only Hawaii. The best time to see fish is early in the morning. Boat tours also bring snorkelers to Molokini during the morning hours, too.

10. Wailua Falls, which is located on the island of Kauai, is one of the most famous waterfalls in the world. The waterfall got some attention when it was featured in the opening credits of the TV series *Fantasy Island*. The falls are also known for how dangerous they are. Ancient Hawaiian men once jumped from the top of the falls in order to prove their manhood. Although jumping off the top of the falls is illegal and dangerous, people still do it today. Back in 2016, a man who jumped from the falls ended up unconscious and nearly died. He was saved when someone swam into the pool to rescue him. Although the pool of water the falls drop into is safe for swimming, swift currents near the waterfall can make it dangerous as well.

11. 'Opaeka'a Falls, which is located near Wailua Falls, is one of the only waterfalls on the island of Kauai that can be seen from the road. It generally falls in a double cascade. The best time to see the falls is on a sunny day. This is when the water gives the appearance of sparkling. *'Opaeka'a* means "rolling shrimp" in Hawaiian, which is a reference to freshwater shrimp that were once plentiful and seen "rolling" down the stream.

12. Sea Life Park on the island of Oahu is an attraction the whole family can enjoy. There's an aquarium, a bird sanctuary that houses sick or injured birds, and a marine mammal park. There are a number of exhibits that may interest marine life lovers, including exhibits that allow you to swim with dolphins, sea lions, and stingrays. There's a sea safari in the aquarium. You can also feed sea turtles. Sea Life Park is also home to a Penguin Habitat. There are a number of shows that take place at the park's Hawaiian Ocean Theater, including dolphins, penguins, and sea lion shows.

13. The Waikiki Aquarium is the second oldest aquarium in the United States. The aquarium was also the first to ever develop displays of living Pacific corals in America. It was the first aquarium to display blacktip reef sharks, broadclub cuttlefish, and the giant clam. The aquarium is also home to a 38-year-old giant clam, which is the oldest giant clam of any aquarium in the world. Founded in 1904, the aquarium is home to more than 3,500 marine animals and plants from over 450 species. The Waikiki Aquarium draws in more than 300,000 visitors each year.

14. Sunset Beach, which is located on the North Shore of Oahu, is a popular place for surfers to

catch big waves during the winter. During the months of summer, the waves are basically nonexistent. In winter, however, they're only ideal for experienced surfers. There are coral formations near the surface, which can be very dangerous for amateur surfers.

15. The Byodo-In Temple, which is located on the island of Oahu, is a non-denominational Buddhist temple. It's a replica of a 900-year-old Buddhist temple in Japan. The temple doesn't have a congregation, but it is visited by thousands of thousands of Buddhist worshippers every year. On the grounds, there are koi ponds. The Byodo-In Temple is a popular place to have weddings.

16. The Waikele Premium Outlets on Oahu are a popular place for tourists to shop. Not only is it home to a number of popular designers, but it's also the only outlet center in Hawaii. Some of the outlets you'll find at the Outlets include Sketchers, Kate Spade, Calvin Klein, Coach, Tommy Hilfiger, Guess, Tory Burch, Sunglass Hut, Godiva, Swarovski, UGG Australia, Zales, Adidas, and the Banana Republic.

17. Shrimp trucks are popular on Hawaii's North Shore. These trucks offer the North Shore's famous garlic shrimp. Romy's is a popular shrimp truck that's a must-try for any tourist.

18. Located in Honolulu, Magic Island is a manmade peninsula. The peninsula was originally created by a resort complex, but it has since been transformed into a park. It's a popular spot for families to picnic and play frisbee. It's also home to festivals and entertainment. Magic Island is also well-known for its Fourth of July fireworks show, which draws in many spectators. The Ala Moana Center, which puts on the fireworks show each year, also offers an Independence Day concert that features a lot of local bands.

19. Puʻuhonua o Hōnaunau National Historical Park is located on the Big Island. The park has an interesting history, which is rich in ancient Hawaiian culture. The park preserves the site where, prior to the early 19th century, Hawaiians once fled when they broke a kapu (or ancient law) in lieu of death. This place of refuge (or *puʻuhonua*) was only an option after the person who broke the kapu was given permission from a priest. The refuge was also a safe haven for defeated warriors and people who didn't want to fight during times of battle. During ancient times, powerful chiefs resided outside the Great Wall that encloses the park.

20. The Halona Blowhole is one of the most popular tourist attractions on Oahu. Located on the east side of the island, the waves crash into the cliffs

under the rocks and causes a blowhole-like surge to fly into the air. It's a great way to cool off.

Test Yourself – Questions and Answers

1. Honolulu is known as the "____ Capital of the World."

   a. Waterfall
   b. Sea turtle
   c. Rainbow

2. The No. 1 most popular tourist attraction in Hawaii is:

   a. Pearl Harbor
   b. Waikiki
   c. The North Shore

3. In Hawaiian, which word means "house of sun"?

   a. Honolulu
   b. Manoa
   c. Haleakala

4. When hiking Mauna Kea, you should stop for how long at the visitor center to prevent altitude sickness?

   a. At least 90 minutes
   b. At least 30 minutes
   c. At least 3 hours

5. The second oldest aquarium in the United States is:

   a. The North Shore Aquarium
   b. Sea Life Park
   c. Waikiki Aquarium

Answers

1. c.

2. a.

3. c.

4. b.

5. c.

CHAPTER SIX

HAWAII'S UNSOLVED MYSTERIES, URBAN LEGENDS, AND OTHER WEIRD FACTS

Have you ever wondered what unsolved mysteries and urban legends haunt the Aloha State? Thanks to the native Hawaiian culture, the state is home to a number of legends. Like other states, Hawaii is also home to quite a few unsolved mysteries. Do you know about Hawaii's legendary "little people"? Have you heard of the goddess who is known to haunt the state? Do you know about the tale of the Ohia tree? Have you heard of the state's first known serial killer? What you read in this chapter might scare you. It might give you goosebumps. Read at your own caution to learn about some of the spookiest tales and most unusual cases surrounding the state.

The Legend of the Volcano Goddess

Are you wondering what you can do to protect yourself and your loved ones from the lava flow the next time there's a volcano eruption? Well, you'll want to keep an eye out for Pele, who, according to native Hawaiian lore, is a volcano goddess.

Some say that in order to stay protected from the volcanoes, you must pay your respects to Pele. If you happen to see the volcano goddess, you'll want to offer her an aloha and also let her know you're willing to help her. Some say that you must visit Pele at the Halemaʻumaʻu crater, where you should offer her food, flowers, or her personal favorite: gin.

If you're wondering what Pele looks like, there are a couple of potential descriptions of the volcano goddess. Some say she's an elderly woman with long, white hair. Others say she's a beautiful woman who has long, flowing hair. It's believed that she can appear in whichever form she wants. Many people claim that Pele is also often seen wearing red.

Local lore says that Pele rewards people who are kind and practice the spirit of "aloha," while punishing those who are selfish and uncaring. It's often said that the old woman version of Pele, presumably in disguise, often knocks on strangers' doors in the middle of the night. She might ask for a cup of tea or water. If you refuse to help her, your family will be affected by bad luck, generally in the form of death or heartbreak. If you help the old woman, however, good luck will fall upon you.

This is all stems from an old Hawaiian tale about the goddess. Once, Pele took the form of an old lady with a cane. She walked to the nearest village and came across a large, luxurious house that had many crops, including taro. When she looked into the window, she saw the family was having a feast. Pele knocked on the door, told them "aloha" and asked if they could spare her some food. She asked for taro, but the family claimed they didn't have enough to share—despite their garden, which was full of taro. She then asked for other food that she knew was plentiful from their garden, and the family said they didn't have enough to share.

Pele continued on her way and came across a smaller house. When she glanced in the window, she saw the family was having a smaller meal. She knocked on the door and said "aloha." She asked this family if they could spare her some food, and they gave her a bowl of poi. Throughout the night, the family shared enough food with the goddess until she was full. They didn't hesitate about sharing. Once Pele was finished, they told her that they didn't have poi until the next harvest.

As a reward for their kindness, Pele made sure they had a fruitful harvest. To punish the first family for their greed, Pele made sure that their crops died.

So, a word of caution: if an old woman asks you for help, just keep in mind that *not* helping her might result in bad fortune.

Pork and the Pali Highway

If you've ever been to Hawaii, you may have heard the saying "you can't take pork over the Pali," but do you know what it means?

This urban legend, which is another one of the many ancient Hawaiian legends involving the volcano goddess, is one of the most well-known in the state.

According to Hawaiian lore, volcano goddess Pele and the half-man, half-pig demigod Kamapua'a broke up and agreed to never visit one another again. If you bring pork over the Pali Highway (which connects Honolulu to the windward side of Oahu), you're symbolically bringing Kamapua'a into Pele's territory.

So, what happens if you bring pork over the Pali? Well, according to Hawaiian lore, Pele will try to stop you. Your car will stop working. To make things creepier, you might come across an old woman who will appear with a dog. You allegedly need to feed the pork to the dog in order to continue on your way.

Pele's Curse

Pele's Curse is another one of the most famous legends involving the volcano goddess. Legend says that if you take rock, sand or any other natural elements from any of the Hawaiian Islands, you will experience bad luck until you return what you have taken.

The thing is, no one actually knows for sure where the legend of Pele's Curse originated from. It's not an ancient legend, meaning it didn't originate from the native Hawaiians. It has been said that a park ranger made it up because he was tired of tourists carrying off rocks while he was working. The myth might have also gotten started by tour guides who wanted to prevent people from bringing sand onto the buses.

Regardless of how it got started, is it possible that the legend could actually be *true*? Hundreds of people send sand, rocks, and other natural minerals they have taken back to the state.

The Kaimuki House

Just about every state has a house that's haunted and Hawaii is no exception. The Kaimuki House is often referred to as the "House of Horrors"—and for good reason!

Located on Harding Avenue and 8th Avenue in Honolulu, there's a house with a goosebumps-inducing past.

The house is believed to be home to a cannibalistic demon that's known as a Kasha. The Kasha, which is similar to a ghoul, is said to feed on the flesh of dead humans. Once it's finished, the Kasha will drag the corpse to Hell.

It all started out when a man allegedly murdered and hid the bodies of his family on the property. While the wife and son's bodies were uncovered, the daughter's body was never found.

In the early 1940s, a woman called the police to report that her children were being assaulted by evil forces. When the police arrived on the scene, they allegedly witnessed the children being tossed across the house… even though there was no one there.

The legend of what happened to the next people to live in the house is far more frightening. The new owners of the house were three sisters. Two of the sisters called the police to report that one of them was grabbed by an evil spirit. The police escorted the sisters from the house and followed after them as they went to their mother's.

On the way their mother's, the sisters pulled their vehicles over to the side of the road. When an officer went to check on the women, they found two of the sisters wrestling an invisible force that appeared to be strangling the third sister. The officer allegedly tried to help but claimed that he was pushed back by a "large calloused hand."

The officer allegedly got the choking woman out of the car. When she went back inside her car, the officer and both of her sisters claimed to witness the door being ripped off and the woman being strangled to death.

Ever since then, there have been countless reports about the unexplained paranormal activity. As a result, no one has stayed in the house for very long.

The Disappearance of Lisa Au

The disappearance of Lisa Au is considered to be one of Hawaii's biggest unsolved mysteries to this day.

Lisa Au was a hairstylist in Kailua on the island of Oahu. She was last seen alive in January of 1982. The night she went missing, she and her boyfriend went to his sister's apartment in Makiki for dinner.

Au's boyfriend said in a 1982 interview that they left dinner around 12:45 a.m. and said goodnight before they left in the separate vehicles they had driven to his sister's apartment.

Her boyfriend discovered her car hours later parked along the highway in Kailua near Kapaa Quarry Road.

Lisa Au was not inside the car.

There was a search for Au through Kawainui Marsh and areas of Kailua, Kaneohe, and Waimanalo.

Au wasn't found during the search.

Two days prior to her disappearance, Lisa Au had

just gotten her driver's license. Her father, Chest Au, had gone with her to buy the car.

When her boyfriend found her empty car, her driver's license and her car registration were both missing. Her purse was still inside the car, however.

Witnesses claimed to have seen a car with blue flashing grill lights behind Au's vehicle. One theory was that someone posing as a police officer—or maybe even an actual police officer—may have been responsible for Au's disappearance.

The Honolulu police department changed their policies. Off-duty police officers were no longer allowed to stop vehicles, and blue grill lights were banned.

Ten days after Lisa Au's car had been found abandoned in Kailua, a jogger and his dog stumbled upon Au's body in Makiki. Au's body was naked and decomposing to the point where the cause of death couldn't be determined.

Even so, Au's death was named a homicide.

No arrests have ever been made in the case.

There have been a number of theories about what happened to Lisa Au. Some people, including Au's parents, believed that the murder was covered up by the police department. Others thought her boyfriend may have been to blame.

The case, which is still considered one of Hawaii's biggest unsolved mysteries, went cold over 30 years ago.

Sadly, Lisa Au's parents have both since passed away, so they will never know who killed their daughter.

The Legend of the Ohia Tree

The Ohia tree's flower is the official flower of the Big Island. The trees are generally the first to grow on new lava flows, making them one of the strongest trees on Hawaii island. If you feel tempted to pick the beautiful red blossoms from an Ohia tree, you might want to think twice.

There's an old Hawaiian legend involving the tree and its flowers. According to lore, Ohia and Lehua were young lovers. Ohia was a handsome young man and Lehua was said to be the most beautiful girl on the Big Island.

One day, however, Pele crossed paths with Ohia and decided she wanted him for himself. When Ohia refused Pele, the volcano goddess turned him into an ugly tree. Lehua begged Pele to change Ohia back. While Pele wouldn't change him back, the other gods felt sorry for Lehua. Although they couldn't undo Pele's magic, the other gods turned Lehua into a beautiful red flower, which they placed on the tree so they would never have to be separated again.

Hawaiian legend has it that picking the pua lehua flowers from the Ohia tree will result in rainfall. This is because it's believed that you'll actually be separating Lehua from Ohia and she won't be able to stop crying. If you leave the flowers on the tree, the weather will stay sunny.

Aliens Have Been Accused of Causing Natural Disasters in Hawaii

Like many other U.S. states, there have been reports of UFO sightings in Hawaii. But did you know that people have questioned if aliens might be responsible for some of Hawaii's natural disasters?

In February of 2018, there were reports of a UFO just *minutes* before not just one but two earthquakes hit Hawaii. To make things more interesting, UFO blogger Nigel Watson, author of the *UFO Investigations Manual*, said that a link between UFO sightings and earthquakes has been found.

This situation wasn't an isolated one in Hawaii, either. In May of 2018, a UFO was spotted hovering over Kilauea on the Big Island as it was erupting. This has prompted some to question if the extraterrestrial activity could be responsible for the volcano's eruption.

Is it possible that aliens could be behind some of

Hawaii's natural disasters? Or are these reported sightings just drones?

The world may never know.

The Legend of the Night Marchers

If you plan to go for any nighttime hikes or walks on the beach, you might want to keep an eye out for the night marchers.

The night marchers are one of the oldest Hawaiian legends. They're said to be the ghosts of ancient warriors who roam the islands during the night hours.

How do you know the difference between a night marcher and any other ghost? Well, they're said to be armed for battle and tend to chant and pound on drums with torches that blaze through the darkness of the night.

Hawaiian lore also says that crossing the patch of night marchers can have some frightening consequences. If you think night marchers might be nearby, your best bet is to go back inside or hide.

If you do end up seeing the night marchers, legend says that you need to either play dead or lie flat at their feet to show your respect. Don't make eye contact with them, though. It's said that anyone who looks into the eyes of a night marcher will be killed unless they share a common ancestor.

The Mystery of the Lost Fisherman

In February of 1979, five men from Hana on the island of Maui left to go fishing on a 17-foot Boston Whaler boat, which was named the "Sarah Joe." All five of the men (Benjamin Kalama, Peter Hanchett, Ralph Malaiakini, Peter Woesner, and Scott Moorman) were experienced fishermen.

The weather was calm that morning, but a storm began to move in by early afternoon. Peter Hanchett's father, John, went to the coast to look for the boat, but it couldn't be found.

The following day, John Hanchett and a marine biologist named John Naughton went to search for the Boston Whaler, but they still turned up nothing.

During the following weeks, people in Hana searched for the Sarah Joe. But there was no trace of the boat.

Then, nearly ten years later, in September of 1988, John Naughton was on a wildlife expedition when he spotted a boat in Taongi of the Marshall Islands, which are located 2,000 miles away from Hawaii. There was a registration number that began with "HA," which led Naughton to believe the boat was registered in Hawaii.

Naughton and his crew stumbled upon a shallow grave near the boat. There was a human jaw bone sticking out of the pile of rocks.

Naughton and his crew contacted the Coast Guard. When they ran the registration number, it was confirmed that the boat was, in fact, the Sarah Joe.

When the grave was excavated, a human skeleton was located. Based on dental records, the skeleton was identified as Scott Moorman. No other skeletal remains were found, but something even more unusual was found buried with the body: a pad of unbound book, with a small square of tin foil between each piece of paper.

To make matters even stranger, there had been no trace of the Sarah Joe in Taongi six years after the men went missing.

This left people asking a lot of questions about the case.

How and when did the boat end up in Taongi?

Who buried Scott Moorman and why did they bury this mysterious pad of paper with him?

Are the other missing fishermen still alive?

The Honolulu Strangler

Did you know that Hawaii was once home to a serial killer?

The Honolulu Strangler is the state's first known serial killer.

The killer was responsible for murdering at least five women between the years of 1985 and 1986. The victims—Vicki Gail Purdy, Regina Sakamoto, Denise Hughes, Louise Medeiros, and Linda Pesce—were between the ages of 17 and 36. All of them had been strangled to death. All of the victims had also been found with their hands bound and had been sexually assaulted.

To date, the Honolulu Strangler hasn't been caught.

It's believed that the killer was an opportunist who attacked women when they alone, such as at bus stops. The killer was also believed to live or work on Sand Island or in Waipahu, which is where the attacks occurred.

Police were led to the body of Linda Pesce, the last known victim, by a 43-year-old man who claimed a psychic told him he would find a body on Sand Island. Police arrested the information as the primary suspect.

The suspect's girlfriend and ex-wife both said he was a smooth talker and that they'd engaged in bondage activity with him, in which they'd allow him to tie their hands behind their backs. To make things stranger, the suspect's girlfriend claimed that he would leave the house on nights they fought, which happened to be the same nights when the murders occurred.

One woman came forward and said that she saw Linda Pesce with a male on the night she was murdered. The woman picked the suspect out of a lineup. She didn't want to be a witness in the case, however.

No other evidence linked the informant to the crime, so he was eventually released.

In 2018, the Honolulu Strangler was featured on *Breaking Homicide* on the *Investigation Discovery* (ID) channel.

The Disappearance of Diane Suzuki

The disappearance of Diane Suzuki is another one of Hawaii's most well-known unsolved mysteries.

Nineteen-year-old Diane Suzuki disappeared in July of 1985. Suzuki, who was a University of Hawaii student, lived in Halawa on Oahu. She was last seen in July of 1985 outside the Rosalie Woodson Dance Academy in Aiea, where she worked part-time as a children's dance instructor.

The day she went missing, Diane Suzuki planned to go to the North Shore with her friends. She was last seen when her class ended. Whenever her friend came to the dance academy fifteen minutes after her class had ended, Diane was gone. Her purse, keys, and the car had all been left behind.

Suzuki's worried parents parked outside the dance studio in case Diane returned. While they were waiting, they witnessed Dewey Hamasaki, who was a photographer who worked at the academy and had a crush on Diane, carry a trunk out of the dance academy. His father and sister helped him carry the trunk, which they placed onto a vehicle.

Dewey Hamasaki, who had been at the studio when Diane Suzuki had finished her lesson, was questioned by the police. He claimed that some scratches he had were caused by a rooster attack. The police searched the marsh around his house, but they didn't turn up anything. Hamasaki was never arrested due to lack of evidence.

Five years after Suzuki went missing, police applied for two search warrants: one for Hamasaki's father's pig farm and one for the dance studio. Only the latter was approved, however.

While traces of blood were found in the dance studio bathroom, they didn't know Diane's blood type for comparison.

Six months later, police were finally approved for the search warrant for the farm. There, they found that a section of a stone wall appeared to have recently been rebuilt—and Hamasaki's father became angry that they focused their attention on it. Hamasaki's father lawyer asked if the prosecutor would be willing to accept a plea bargain if the suspects pled guilty to manslaughter. The prosecutor rejected the offer in hopes of finding evidence of murder.

During the investigation, the stump of a banana tree was removed and the ground was dug up. This uncovered clothes that looked like what Diane had been last seen wearing... and the clothing was also her size.

Tests indicated that the stone wall had only been built six months prior to the investigation. It was theorized that the delay in acquiring the search warrant gave the Hamasaki's time to hide Suzuki's body.

In 1993, the case was presented to three investigative grand juries, but the court declined to press charges for lack of evidence. The investigation ended then.

Dewey Hamasaki remains a photographer. He has since published a Christian photography book.

The Rosalie Dance Academy remains open.

Hamasaki's funeral took place in 1997, even though her body was never found. Her mother passed away the following year.

While Dewey Hamasaki has always been the prime suspect in the case, some have questioned if Diane Suzuki's disappearance may have been the work of the Honolulu Strangler, who murdered his victims during the same time period. While police didn't believe there was anything that tied Suzuki to the Honolulu Strangler, her body was never found to know for sure.

The Legend of the Menehune

This urban legend is, by far, one of the most famous legends of Hawaii. Most states have legends about "little people." The Hawaiian version of these people is called "Menehune."

While people have called the Menehune Hawaii's version of Bigfoot, the two are actually opposites. While Bigfoot is, well, *big*, the Menehune are thought to be dwarf-like people, who are estimated to be about two feet tall. They're what you might consider to be the Hawaiian version of fairies or Ireland's leprechauns.

The Menehune are said to be mischievous beings who often play pranks on islanders. They're believed to live in Hawaii's forests and valleys where they hide away from humans. According to lore, the Menehune lived in Hawaii before the first Polynesian settlers. Ancient Hawaiian texts say that the Menehune drove out the Nawao, who, according to legends, was a group of large hunters who lived in the wild.

The Menehune are believed to possess the ability to build anything they want within 24 hours. But don't catch them while they're building something. The Menehune, who are known to be very shy, prefer to work at night so that they won't have interactions with humans. If a human does catch them while they're working, the Menehune will stop whatever it is they're working on and never come back to finish it. Meanwhile, the person who interrupted their work will be turned to stone.

Ancient Hawaiian legend says that they created the Menehune Fish Pond and the Menehune Ditch on Kauai.

Although this urban legend might sound far-fetched, some historians actually believe it could be true. They believe the Menehune were people from Marquesas Island who migrated to the Big Island of Hawaii prior to the Tahitians. The Tahitians may have forced the Menehune to migrate deeper into the forest for their survival.

One of the signs that a Menehune may be nearby is the sound of splashing near a beach or waterfall during nighttime hours. In addition to building things and causing mischief, the Menehune are known to love diving.

While many historians believe that the Menehune are the result of legends shared when the natives had contact with Europeans, there are reported sightings of the mythical beings to this day.

There's Said to Be a Portal to the Afterlife in Hawaii

Have you ever wondered how the deceased travel to the afterlife?

Rumor has it that Ka'ena Point is a portal between our world and the afterlife. According to local lore, however, it doesn't work for those who are already alive. The portal can only be accessed by those who have already died.

It's the one spot on the island of Oahu where spirits—or *uhane* in Hawaiian—need to go if they want to leave our world. A uhane is said to be able to do this by jumping into the other realm. If they get lost and are unable to make the jump, it's said that the uhane will be forced to haunt the island until it can eventually find its way to the next realm.

The Secret of Where King Kamehameha I's Bones Are Buried

One of Hawaii's best-kept secrets is where King Kamehameha I's bones are buried.

Ancient Hawaiians had a burial ritual known as *hunakele*, which means "to hide in secret." The process involved extracting the flesh from the bones, which was later followed by a secret burial of the bones. Generally, in cases of "sacred" bones (such as that of a King or another Ali'i), only one chief knew the details of the burial site. This was partly for safekeeping and to help the deceased make a peaceful transition to the world of the gods or *aumakua*. But another reason for this secrecy in ancient Hawaiian burials is because it was believed that if an enemy came into contact with the bones, the deceased's chiefly *mana*, or power, would be transferred to them.

King Kamehameha died on May 8th, 1819, and since then, many have wondered where his bones are buried. The location of the King's bones was kept secret by Chief Ulumaheihei, who was entrusted with the details of the burial. The bones were hidden at night, which is common with the hunakele.

It's believed that King Kamehameha I's bones are located inside of a burial cave at Kaloko-Honokohau National Historic Park, which is located on the Big Island of Hawaii. Other famous rulers, including King Kahekili of Maui, are also thought to be buried in the cave. It has also been rumored that Kamehameha's bones may have been moved to the Royal Mausoleum in Oahu's Nu'uanu Valley on Oahu, at King Kalakaua's request. However, no one has ever confirmed for sure where Kamehameha's bones are buried. It's remained a secret since 1819, so it seems safe to say that no one will spill the beans anytime soon!

The Iolani Palace May Also Be Haunted

The Iolani Palace, which is one of Oahu's most famous historical landmarks, has been the source of a number of reports of paranormal activity. There have been numerous reports of unexplained voices, footsteps, odors, apparitions, and shadowy figures.

One of the palace's most well-known spirits is that of a water ghost. The ghost allegedly leaves his wet footprints down the hallways. Many believe that the ghost is that of a Hawaiian prince who was dunked in water as a form of punishment. The water dunking caused him to develop pneumonia, which he died from.

Another one of Iolani Palace's ghost is a woman in white. She's said to roam the grounds at night. People have reported hearing her crying outside the palace. The woman in white then vanishes near the stairs that run under the palace's fountain.

Reports of strange paranormal incidents at the palace are so common that no one even bats an eye when people mention unusual sightings.

RANDOM FACTS

1. Due to its tragic history, it might not surprise you to learn that Pearl Harbor is believed to be one of the most haunted spots in the country. There are often reports of apparitions of soldiers on the dock of one of the sunken vessels, and that's not all: people also report feelings of unexplained pain and feelings of fear.

2. Hickman Air Force Base, which also experienced the effects of Pearl Harbor on December 7th, 1941, is also thought to be haunted. An alarming number of strange occurrences have happened since the tragedy took place. People have reportedly heard the sounds of bombs exploding and soldiers dying. There have also been reports of World War II soldiers' apparitions wandering the base.

3. The naupaka plant can be found throughout Hawaii's beaches and mountains. The plant is known for its flower, which looks like they're torn in half. An old Hawaiian legend says that Naupaka was a beautiful princess who fell in love with a guy named Kaui, who was just a commoner. Their different social classes prevented them from ever being able to marry.

Since they were forbidden from being together, they chose to live far away from one another, with Naupaka staying in the mountains and Kaui living along the ocean. But before the star-crossed lovers said goodbye, Naupaka removed the flower she wore in her hair and tore it in half. She kept half of it for herself and gave the other half to Kaui. As the tale goes, the lovers' parting devastated the flowers so much that they went on to only produce half-flowers in honor of the tragic love story.

4. Hanalei, Kauai resident Nancy Ellen Baugh disappeared in June of 1979. Witnesses claimed to have seen Baugh being dragged out of a house, screaming, in the middle of the night. Someone sent anonymous letters to Baugh's family after she went missing. Nancy Ellen Baugh's body was found in 2013 in the Waioli Stream during a flood, but police were never able to figure out what happened to her.

5. In Japanese folklore, the obake is a shape-shifter. (*Obake* means "a thing that changes" in Japanese). The term is commonly used to describe a number of different types of supernatural beings in Hawaii, including ghosts. One of the most well-known obake is the Green Lady. She's a woman who's said to be covered in moss and green mold. Some say she has green scales that resemble that

of a fish, jagged teeth, and seaweed-covered hair. The Green Lady allegedly wanders the Wahiawa gulch. People have reported seeing the Green Lady near the Wahiawa Botanical Garden, as well as the Wahiawa Elementary School. According to local lore, the Green Lady was a woman who visited the Wahiawa gulch with her kids. While they were there, one of her children disappeared and was never seen again. The woman allegedly died of a broken heart. Now, her spirit roams the area in search of her lost child. But be careful! The Green Lady is said to take any lonely children she stumbles upon.

6. During construction that was done on Highway 1, which runs through the Koolau Mountains in Oahu, something eerie was uncovered. Excavation workers found the bones of ancient warriors. It got creepier when workers claimed to see apparitions and hear the warriors' voices speak to them. Other people have reportedly heard the sound of the warriors crying inside the highway tunnels.

7. The Iao Theatre in Wailuku on Maui is said to be haunted. The theatre, which opened in 1928, is said to be home to a number of paranormal occurrences. There have been reports of strange shadowy figures, unexplained coldness, and unusual voices. People have reported seeing the

apparition of a female ghost who wanders around the theatre's seating and stage. Don't worry, though—she's said to be friendly. There have also been claims of ghosts of Hawaiian soldiers in the theatre basement.

8. Old Pali Road in Nuuanu Valley on Oahu is said to be haunted. The most well-known spirit that haunts the road is believed to be that of a young girl, who's missing half her face. Some say she has long, raven-black hair and that she often skips down the road. She allegedly has rope marks around her neck and the only facial feature she has are two bulging eyes. Rumor has it that the ghost is that of a girl who was raped and later strangled to death with a jump rope and was then hidden along the road. According to local lore, animals ate part of her face before her severely decomposed body was found and that's why her ghost is missing half her face.

9. Morgan's Corner, which is located along Old Pali Road, is also said to be haunted. It's a curve in the road that can be easily be found thanks to the giant tree that marks it. The tree is allegedly the source of much paranormal activity. Some claim that they've seen the apparitions of people hanging from the tree, while others claim to hear unexplained sounds on the roof of their car when it's dark out.

10. It was once said that Hawaii has never had Bigfoot sightings. While this couldn't be further from the truth, there haven't been nearly as many as most states. Hawaii is also said to have its own "Bigfoot." The creature is known as an "Aikanaka." The ape-like beast is said to resemble a man. It stands about 8 feet tall and has shaggy hair. The Aikanaka is thought to live in highly forested areas and has reportedly startled drivers on isolated roads. There are alleged sightings to this day, but many believe the Aikanaka to be just another urban legend.

11. A couple was found dead on the Kuilau Ridge Trail on the island of Kauai back in 1981. The couple, John and Michelle Klein, were tourists who were visiting the state from California. They had been shot, but their personal belongings had been left unturned. The *Associated Press* published an article about the murders in 1982, which suggested that the Klein's had been killed because they'd stumbled on nearly a ton of weed within a mile of where their bodies had been found.

12. The Hilton Hawaiian Village on Oahu is said to be haunted. According to local lore, one of the hotel's employees witnessed a woman vanish, never to be seen again. Rumor has it that the woman may have been murdered in her hotel

room. Another one of the hotel's most famous ghosts is a woman in a red dress. She's allegedly been seen wandering the hotel halls and the beach. Some believe the woman in red is actually Pele, the volcano goddess. This doesn't seem too far-fetched since Pele seems to be all over the state.

13. People often report sightings of Queen Liliuokalani at the capitol building. One of the most well-known reports came from State Senator Eloise Tungpalan's then 10-year-old daughter. Senator Tungpalan took her daughter to the office. Her daughter claimed she made a friend who she described as a tall Hawaiian who wore leis and a long dress and was barefoot. No one else met the girl's friend, but when she saw the Queen Liliuokalani statue at the capitol building, the girl recognized it as her friend. But Senator Tungpalan's daughter isn't the only one who's seen the ghost of Queen Liliuokalani. Both locals and tourists have made reports of seeing her apparition. Queen Liliuokalani was known to love to smoke cigars while she was alive, and people often claim to smell the odor cigars lingering in the air after reported sightings.

14. The Lodge at Koele, which is located in Lanai, appears to be a beautiful resort at first glance. It might surprise you to learn that the resort is one

of the most famously haunted hotels in all of Hawaii! There are a number of spirits that are said to reside at the resort, including the ghost of a little girl who is often spotted wandering in guest's rooms. The strangest part about it all is that there are no known tragedies that may explain how the resort got to be so haunted.

15. It has been said that a "drowning spirit" haunts the falls and lagoon of the Waimea Valley Falls. In fact, it's even been rumored that the spirit is why tourists are no longer allowed to swim in the area. Only trained divers are allowed to dive the area. Whether or not this is true, the drowning spirit looks for humans to sacrifice. The spirit is said to drown a human, which it will keep until it decides to release it to the surface. The spirit traces back to more than 50 years. Back in 1952, a sailor named Bill Lawrence drowned in the lagoon. His friends witnessed him struggling. He would swim back to the surface before dragged back under, they claimed. Tragically, his friends were unable to get to him in time. After it was evident that he'd drowned, they decided to remain in the area until his body was found. They claimed to hear the sounds of people running back and forth from the lagoon to the woods and back again throughout the night. Lawrence's dead body was located the following day.

16. Many people throughout Hawaii have reported encounters with what is known as "The Choking Ghost." This ghost comes to you in the middle of the night, presses on your chest, and chokes you. It's impossible to scream or move. Just as you believe you're about to suffocate, the ghost leaves. Some believe this strange phenomenon may be caused by sleep paralysis, but others think evil spirits are to blame.

17. The Oahu Community Correctional Facility, which is the largest jail in the state, is believed to be haunted. The jail, which was once known as the Oahu Prison. Between the years of 1909 and 1944, men were hung from the prison's gallows. Prisoners have claimed to witness unusual paranormal activity at the facility, including cell doors rattling on their own. Even guards have made claims of paranormal activity, which allegedly happens frequently in the squad room.

18. The Honolulu Airport is said to be haunted by the Lady in Waiting. The story goes like this: she was once a woman who fell in love with a man who claimed he wished to marry her. The wedding never happened, however. He took a flight from the Honolulu Airport, from which he never returned. The Lady in Waiting was so brokenhearted that she committed suicide. Her spirit, which wears a white dress, is now said to

wander the airport, hopelessly waiting for him to return so they can get married.

19. The Wainapanapa cave on Maui is the source of an ancient Hawaiian legend. As the story goes, Princess Popo'alaea hid in the cave from her jealous and coldhearted husband, Chief Ka'akea. Chief Ka'akea eventually found and killed her. The waters of the cave turn red a few times a year, which is believed to be in honor of the princess.

20. Since the 1980s, there have been reports of sightings of a big wild cat that is described to have deer colored skin and a long tail. Based on these descriptions, it seems safe to assume that the wildcat might be a cougar. Between 2002 and 2003, there were eight reports of the cat in the Olinda district of Maui. Authorities theorized that someone's exotic pet had managed to escape and was roaming free. Searches and attempts at capturing the cat turned up nothing in 2003. The cat has since been known as "The Maui Mystery Cat." After a pet fawn was found mauled, Hawaii state officials called in a big expert named Bill Van Pelt to try to find the cat. While Van Pelt didn't locate the cat and was unable to obtain video footage, he did find tracks and claw marks that indicated there was a big cat in the area. DNA analysis was done on hair that was found,

but the results proved to be inconclusive. After 2003, reports of the Maui Mystery Cat became less frequent.

Test Yourself – Questions and Answers

1. The case that's regarded as one of Hawaii's biggest unsolved mysteries to date is:

    a. The disappearance of Nancy Ellen Baugh
    b. The disappearance of Queen Liliuokalani
    c. The disappearance of Lisa Au

2. The name of Hawaii's first known serial killer is:

    a. The Honolulu Hanger
    b. The Honolulu Strangler
    c. The Honolulu Killer

3. Which of the following is _not_ a form Pele, the volcano goddess, is believed to take?

    a. An old woman
    b. A woman in red
    c. A woman missing half her face

4. Hawaii's "little people" are known as:

    a. Menehune
    b. Obake
    c. Aikanaka

5. It's believed that ____ might be responsible for some of Hawaii's natural disasters.

    a. Bigfoot
    b. Drowning spirits
    c. Aliens

Answers

1. c.
2. b.
3. b.
4. a.
5. c.

DON'T FORGET YOUR FREE BOOKS

GET THEM FOR FREE ON
WWW.TRIVIABILL.COM

OTHER BOOKS IN THIS SERIES

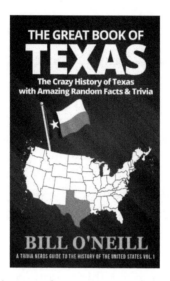

Are you looking to learn more about Texas? Sure, you've heard about the Alamo and JFK's assassination in history class, but there's so much about the Lone Star State that even natives don't know about. In this trivia book, you'll journey through Texas's history, pop culture, sports, folklore, and so much more!

In The Great Book of Texas, some of the things you will learn include:

Which Texas hero isn't even from Texas?

Why is Texas called the Lone Star State?

Which hotel in Austin is one of the most haunted hotels in the United States?

Where was Bonnie and Clyde's hideout located?

Which Tejano musician is buried in Corpus Christi?

What unsolved mysteries happened in the state?

Which Texas-born celebrity was voted "Most Handsome" in high school?

Which popular TV show star just opened a brewery in Austin?

You'll find out the answers to these questions and many other facts. Some of them will be fun, some of them will creepy, and some of them will be sad, but all of them will be fascinating! This book is jampacked with everything you could have ever wondered about Texas.

Whether you consider yourself a Texas pro or you know absolutely nothing about the state, you'll learn something new as you discover more about the state's past, present, and future. Find out about things that weren't mentioned in your history book. In fact, you might even be able to impress your history teacher with your newfound knowledge once you've finished reading! So, what are you waiting for? Dive in now to learn all there is to know about the Lone Star State!

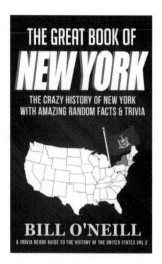

Want to learn more about New York? Sure, you've heard about the Statue of Liberty, but how much do you really know about the Empire State? Do you know why it's even called the Empire State? There's so much about New York that even state natives don't know. In this trivia book, you'll learn more about New York's history, pop culture, folklore, sports, and so much more!

In The Great Book of New York, you'll learn the answers to the following questions:

- Why is New York City called the Big Apple?
- What genre of music started out in New York City?
- Which late actress's life is celebrated at a festival held in her hometown every year?
- Which monster might be living in a lake in New York?

- Was there really a Staten Island bogeyman?
- Which movie is loosely based on New York in the 1800s?
- Which cult favorite cake recipe got its start in New York?
- Why do the New York Yankees have pinstripe uniforms?

These are just a few of the many facts you'll find in this book. Some of them will be fun, some of them will be sad, and some of them will be so chilling they'll give you goosebumps, but all of them will be fascinating! This book is full of everything you've ever wondered about New York.

It doesn't matter if you consider yourself a New York state expert or if you know nothing about the Empire State. You're bound to learn something new as you journey through each chapter. You'll be able to impress your friends on your next trivia night!

So, what are you waiting for? Dive in now so you can learn all there is to know about New York!

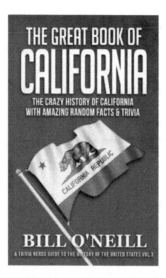

Are you interested in learning more about California? Sure, you've heard of Hollywood, but how much do you really know about the Golden State? Do you know how it got its nickname or what it was nicknamed first? There's so much to know about California that even people born in the state don't know it all. In this trivia book, you'll learn more about California's history, pop culture, folklore, sports, and so much more!

In The Great Book of California, you'll discover the answers to the following questions

- Why is California called the Golden State?
- What music genres started out in California?
- Which celebrity sex icon's death remains a mystery?
- Which serial killer once murdered in the state?

- Which childhood toy started out in California?
- Which famous fast-food chain opened its first location in the Golden State?
- Which famous athletes are from California?

These are just a few of the many facts you'll find in this book. Some of them will be entertaining, some of them will be tragic, and some of them may haunt you, but all of them will be interesting! This book is full of everything you've ever wondered about California and then some!

Whether you consider yourself a California state expert or you know nothing about the Golden State, you're bound to learn something new in each chapter. You'll be able to impress your college history professor or your friends during your next trivia night!

What are you waiting for? Get started to learn all there is to know about California!

MORE BOOKS BY BILL O'NEILL

I hope you enjoyed this book and learned something new. Please feel free to check out some of my previous books. on Amazon.